T0087963

On ADMIRATION

Also by W. D. Wetherell

A Century of November
Soccer Dad
North of Now
Hills like White Hills

On *Admiration*

heroes, heroines, role models, and mentors

W. D. Wetherell

Skyhorse Publishing

Skyhorse Publishing books may be purchased in bulk at special
discounts for sales promotion, corporate gifts, fund-raising, or educational
purposes. Special editions can also be created to specifications. For details,
contact the Special Sales Department, Skyhorse Publishing,
555 Eighth Avenue, Suite 903, New York, NY 10018 or
info@skyhorsepublishing.com.

www.skyhorsepublishing.com

10 9 8 7 6 5 4 3 2 1

Library of Congress Cataloging-in-Publication Data

Wetherell, W. D., 1948-
On admiration : heroes, heroines, role models, and mentors / W. D.
Wetherell.
p. cm.
ISBN 978-1-61608-071-6 (hbk. : alk. paper)
1. Wetherell, W. D., 1948---Childhood and youth. 2. Wetherell, W. D.,
1948---Knowledge--Celebrities. 3. Heroes. 4. Role models. I. Title.
PS3573.E9248Z46 2010
813'.54--dc22
[B]
                                    2010020239

Printed in China

For my mother and father,
in admiring memory

Contents

Introduction

I intend to brag only once in these pages, and I'm going to do it in the following sentence: No book quite like this one has ever been attempted before. All the more reason to try and explain how it first came about.

Last November, on what used to be called Armistice Day, I saw a photo in our newspaper of the folksinger Pete Seeger—an elderly Pete Seeger with an infantryman's cap on, not singing or taking part in a demonstration, but gathering with other World War II vets for his town's annual parade. Pete Seeger, the living legend. Pete Seeger, who had outlasted all his critics, all those who tried to muzzle him. Pete Seeger, who, when I was fourteen, I admired greatly, to the point where I bought all his albums and memorized his songs, this at a time when all my friends were listening to The Beatles or Petula Clark. I found the photo, and what it stirred in my memory, to be tremendously moving—so much so that I decided to sit down and sketch out a nostalgic essay about the role Seeger had played in my young life.

That same week, my then-fourteen-year-old son Matthew received a remarkable piece of snail mail from New Zealand. He collects autographs, mostly sports stars, but occasionally from survivors of the all-but-vanished past. He had gotten one from Max Schmeling in Germany, almost certainly among the last the famous old heavyweight signed before his death. Now, when he carefully opened the envelope, he found one that was even more special: the autograph of Edmund Hillary, the first person to climb Everest fifty years before. Touching a piece of paper he had touched, seeing his bold, confident signature—*Ed Hillary*—thinking how generous it was of him to reply to a boy's query half a world away—all this excited me even more than it did Matthew, and got me explaining to him how when I was his age, Sir Edmund Hillary had been one of my greatest heroes.

Two nudges now, two little proddings. The third, the one that completed the process and got me started, was my daughter Erin calling from college to say they were reading Willa Cather's *My Antonia*—my favorite novel from one of my all-time favorite novelists. I had gone through a real Cather phase as a young writer, which overlapped my Conrad phase and my Chekhov phase and even my Proust phase, to the point where the mere mention of those names—as my daughter found out during our phone conversation—could get me raving on and on about their miraculous and inspiring art.

In short, there came a point this past year when I realized that I had greatly admired a good many people in the course of my life—not just relatives or friends (although I admired plenty of those), but heroes and heroines from the larger world, some famous and celebrated by almost everyone, others obscure and forgotten except to me. People who had entertained me, inspired me, educated me, consoled me—men and women who had enlarged my appreciation of beauty, sharpened my courage, made me feel honored to be their fellow human, served as my role models and mentors. Further, as a writer, I'm always looking for a challenge—some new and difficult way to frame experience—and so out of these converging threads, a question started gnawing away at my habitual inertia and reluctance, to the point where I began thinking about it constantly.

Was it possible, I wondered, for a person to tell his or her life story exclusively in terms of who they had admired in the larger world, and why? Possible to write a memoir, not in terms of the usual autobiographical fodder, but by praising the heroes and heroines who inhabited your own personal pantheon of greats? Possible to reveal your innermost self by writing not a confession, but a celebration?

I believe it is possible. "We live by our admirations," Emerson said—and his aphorism is the guiding principle behind this memoir.

Another, more confessional motive is at work here: My own life is *not* one that lends itself to a conventional autobiography. No novelist was ever born into a drabber, more nonliterary environment, nor, growing to maturity, remained so solitary in habits and conservative in lifestyle. No rags to riches in my story, no epic drinking bouts, no scintillating amours—the turmoil in my life has all been internal. My autobiography could be written in a single, long sentence: I had a happy, conventional suburban childhood, followed by a discouraging, despairing late adolescence, capped off by an autodidactic period in my late teens and early twenties of torturously difficult reinvention, then a long apprenticeship trying to get a grip on my imagination, leading to grudging success, the never-ending roller coaster of exhilarating triumph followed by abject failure, marrying late, moving to the country, and the miracle of kids. Boring stuff for a book—a man who is too bohemian to be bourgeois and too bourgeois to be a bohemian, carving out a life for himself in that unexciting, unexamined, unexplainable no-man's-land that lays unpublished in between.

That would be my standard autobiography, the one there's no use writing. In the experimental one, it's all quite different. In that one, I hobnob with the greats, cavort among the immortals, philosophize with them, swap stories, trade puns, march to their drumbeat, play ball with them, sing, ponder, paint—in other words, live the dramatic, colorful, inspiring, anecdote-filled life of pure admiration.

So it's a memoir I'm writing—but a natural history, too. Admiration as a human emotion has seldom been fully charted or described. This is especially true in this celebrity-ridden age, where "I like so-and-so" is said all the time, and "I admire so-and-so," hardly ever. The difference in verbs speaks volumes. We "like" our favorite band, actor, or politician the same way we "like" a certain kind of soda or beer; it's a sort of fast, easy branding we can use in lieu of any deeper self-characterization. As mentors to model our behavior on, guide us, inspire us, expand our sense of possibility, we hardly take celebrities seriously at all, the convenient thing about brands being their disposability. "Oh—I like so-and-so" implies, in our age, that we can easily forget them.

Admiration is one of the "social emotions" that psychologists still find mysterious—at least when it comes to our internal wiring. According to the lead authors of a recent study at the Brain and Creativity Institute: "The neural basis of admiration has not been investigated." They then proceed to take a crack at it, since, after all, "admiration is arguably one of the most refined feelings in the human repertoire." After many clever experiments, in which they differentiate between admiration for virtue (AV) and admiration for skill (AS), they find that "admiration engages subcortical nuclei in brainstem and hypo-thalamus [sic], and somatosensory cortices in interoceptive and extero-ceptive sectors, including the superio [sic] parietal lobule and suprama-rginal gyrus." Which is to say, like so many other emotions, admiration has scientists hot on its trail.

Admiration, as an emotion, has been on the decline at least since the 1960s. Writing toward the end of that decade, essayist Edward Hoagland (whom I admire) had some prescient things to say about the subject, pointing to Kennedy's assassination as a real turning point:

> We kill our heroes nowadays, as too much admiration fixes upon them, a killer emerges, representing more than just himself. Afraid of what will happen if we admire someone too much, we look a little to one side, taking care to hedge our praise until, like other feelings that go unsaid too long, it loses immediacy . . . The very character of admiration has changed, we have no tolerance now. One slip and we will damn some-body forever.

Albert Schweitzer is damned, Hoagland points out, because of our agnosticism; Albert Einstein gets short shrift because we dread the results of his scientific discoveries. "We're sick of anti-heroes, too," Hoagland writes, which leaves us at a loss, since: "It's not as if we don't still need heroes. They dramatize solutions and help to pave the way through new circumstances; they stumble on a stance that suits nearly everybody . . . Heroes embody aspirations that we ourselves share, or remember fondly, and to be cored of our heroes is to be cored of aspirations."

The sixties debunked admiration, and people in the future might not have much time for it either. The psychologists who study admira-tion go to great lengths to explain that the brain's ancient bioregula-tory structures, when it comes to something as refined as admiration, can't be rushed. They worry that, when it comes to admiration, "the rapidity and parallel processing of attention-requiring information, which hallmark the digital age, might reduce the frequency of full experience of such emotions, with potentially negative consequences," or, in other words, the Internet might be too fast to let our brains admire anyone we find on it.

As will become apparent, I grew up in something of a golden age of admiration, before cynicism took hold. There was enough high-tech around (television, radio, hi-fidelity records) to create a pool of potential admirer-ees from which even a boy living in the capital village of world philistinism could choose. At the same time, it still seemed perfectly reasonable for a young person to look to the past to find his or her heroes—through books and the stories of his parents—through a kind of collective cultural memory that wasn't yet extinct. The past is the very last place most young people would think to look for heroes and heroines today, but in my childhood, at least to those of us who fell in love with reading, it seemed a most obvious direction. Old tech supplied what new tech didn't. Between them, the raw material of admiration had never been in greater supply.

So, put that down as this book's not-so-secret agenda: to try and restore admiration to its rightful place as one of the most honorable and enjoyable of all human emotions—to reestablish admiration, not just as an emotion, but as an art. It will also serve, almost despite itself, as a cultural history of the last sixty years, showing what one representative member of his generation found in his culture worth worshipping, and, by the unimpeachable evidence of his silence, who he found worth ignoring completely.

Admiration is said to be a passive emotion, dismissed as the fodder of fan clubs, but I've never found this to be true. Admiration, at its most intense, floods over you like a wave, carries you in a direction you might not be prepared to go just then, takes you to a strange new shore that, in the end, turns out to be one that makes all the difference. Admiration leads to emulation, which is anything but passive; the mentors described in this book, almost every one of them, stirred me to action, if only in my thoughts and dreams. And the heroes worshipped were anything but passive themselves; whether writers, singers, statesmen, or actors, they spent their careers reaching out for an audience or a following, actively searching for admirers, sympathizers, acolytes, and converts. So, in a very real sense, my yearning met their yearning halfway.

Many of those I'll honor here have written memoirs of their own; there is a huge supply of testament available explaining what it's like to be "great," whether it be as a novelist, politician, or a singer, but very little written from the other side of the collaboration, by the solitary admirer out there who finds their work, absorbs it, brings it to life. Is Giuseppe Verdi a great composer even if no one is listening to his music? Leo Tolstoy an immortal writer if his works go unread? Art, even entertainment, is a collaboration, and it's high time we heard from the receptive, supposedly "passive" half of that partnership.

One caution to keep in mind: Admiration is similar to all the other human emotions in that it can lead us badly astray. Compiling a list of lifetime heroes can be an embarrassing project, if it's honest, since so many of our idols turn out, retrospectively, to have feet of clay. Fashions in heroes often change; the politically honored of one age become the politically incorrect of another, to say nothing of the cynical debunking of reputations history is so good at. The temptation to prune and censor your list is a strong one—but I'm going to resist it here, and if it's a bit embarrassing to have once admired someone called Bernard "Boom Boom" Geoffrion, well, any memoirist has moments where they blush. If anything, I still remain surprisingly loyal to all of my admirations; they contributed to who I am, and I can forgive them for their human frailties. There's a warts-and-all, tough-love, tell-it-like-it-is aspect in my approach; it's important to remember that paying homage does not mean kissing ass. It's admiration I'm talking about in these pages, not adulation.

Every person written about here deserves an entire book—or at least a chapter—devoted to celebrating their talent. Instead, I will have to move fast in order to get everyone in, hoping that I can suggest the pageant-like quality they've had in my life. It's a parade of varied talents that I admire, and quite often one hero links arms with another; sometimes, they even march three abreast. Then, too, I have to devote space to my many minor heroes and heroines, as they're part of the parade as well.

If I look at my notes, I see that I've written down the names of approximately forty people whose talents and virtues I'd like to celebrate. Many of them are widely known; some are known only to specialists; one or two hardly anyone has ever been aware of but me.

Approximately fifteen of these I saw in person at one time or another; two I shook hands with; one I actually met and became friends with; five or six were connected to me by one thin degree of separation. The biggest grouping is writers; the second-biggest, composers and singers; but artists, actors, politicians, and athletes are included as well. Several are fictional heroes who became very real to me. Most are dead white men—but if I added those people in my personal life I've admired most, or the public personalities I'm increasingly drawn to as I get older, the list would be heavily weighted toward females. Many of the people I worshipped were leading me to reexamine my culture, to break away from it if I found the courage—but even with their heavy influence, I am a product of my culture and times, and what that culture had on offer, for too many years, was dead white males.

There is one great debatable question this memoir will not directly address, although the implications are inherent in every line. If a book can be crafted out of pure admiration, does that mean, in the end, that mankind is admirable? "Is the world upheld," as Emerson put it, "by the veracity of good men?" I'm writing in perilous times, a moment in history when man, judging by the headlines, is particularly despicable. Do our "good humans" redeem all the horror that goes down? Do they make up for the tyrants, the sleaze merchants, the power-crazed and greedy, the dogmatic, the liars, the torturers, the slick?

I can sidestep the question temporarily—it's early pages yet, and I haven't sunk my teeth far enough into admiration to answer either way. But if you were to make me hazard a guess here at the start, I'd hem and haw a bit, stare off into the middle distance, remember those people who inspired me at the moment in life when I most needed them, and answer—diffidently, adding on all kinds of qualifiers, doubts, exceptions—that there is at least some evidence, the evidence included in these pages, that mankind *is* admirable, and the men and women I write about here have gifted us with an honor and dignity that horror can tarnish but never completely corrode.

On ADMIRATION

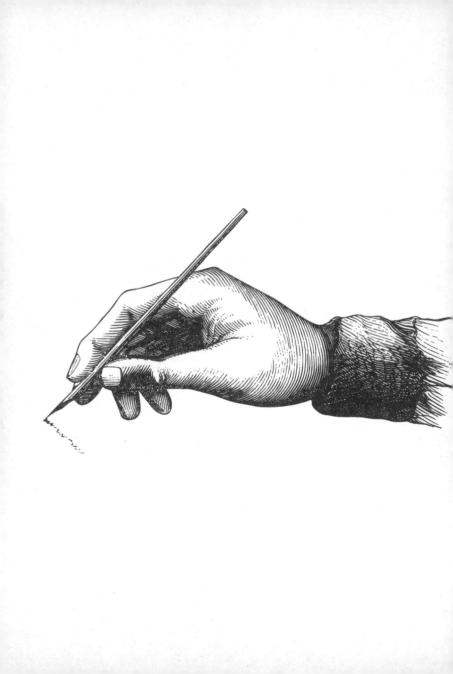

PART ONE

Pure Admiration

DWIGHT D. EISENHOWER

Liked Ike? The boy loved him. Loved him with all the uncritical, nondiscriminatory zeal of an ardent six-year-old heart. Loved him like he loved his mother, father, and sister Christina. Loved him like he loved his grandparents, Aunt Addy, Aunt Lyd, and Uncle Joe. Loved him like he loved his Sunday school teacher, or Miss D'Amato, his kindergarten teacher. Loved him like he did Mr. Kelscy at the hardware store, who could scoop up a half-pound's worth of gray penny nails in one fist, weigh them on his metal cradle, and not be off by more than one or two nails. Loved him like Mr. Costa, the butcher who would always slice him off a piece of bologna when his mother took him there after the baker's. Loved him like he loved Taffy, the family cocker spaniel, which is saying quite a lot.

For Ike was almost certainly the first public face he had ever learned to recognize, one beaming down from a much-larger world than the cozy Long Island neighborhood that snugly bound him in. Subtract all the thousands of public faces he would eventually see in newspapers, movies, or on TV, and the face that was there at the start was Eisenhower's, the Big Bang of all faces, the one out of which, by some magic, all the other public faces seemed to be generated. Truman was president when he was born, true, but the only thing he remembered about Truman was his mother, who was no prude, making a bad-smell kind of expression and saying, "Such language! And from a president!"

Ike didn't swear or cuss. Ike spoke surprisingly fast, in a clipped military tone that to the boy seemed exotic, even exquisite, compared to the guttural New Yorkese all the adults he knew spoke. And that face! He was far from being the only one enchanted by it. There was God in Ike's smile, the New Testament God you prayed to for favors, but there was also something earthier—the smile of a beloved old family doctor dispensing reassuring advice. And there was even more magic than that, magic that perhaps was lost on the millions who voted for him, but was perfectly obvious to the boy. A baby's innocence lay behind Ike's smile, at least if you focused on his pinkish dimple and chin (even in black and white, they looked pink). Eisenhower, over sixty now, smiled like an eight-month-old—and what boy, so close to babyhood himself, could resist that fraternal appeal?

"Dear Ike in heaven, look down from above," he would sometimes begin his prayers at night. His parents, busy tucking in his blankets, never noticed the mistake.

This was 1954. Approbation was in the air and the boy quickly succumbed. Why shouldn't he? The human capacity for admiration grows even faster than a child's arms and legs, and very quickly needs something to fasten on to in order to strengthen. Parents will do for a time, older siblings, kindly aunts and uncles—but there comes the moment when you need someone distant, someone who is clean of all the little nicks and dents admiration suffers when its object is too close at hand, too human, too apt to scold. Admiration, in a six-year-old, is a surprisingly strong muscle, and it tends to grasp the most obvious hero the culture has on offer.

Ike filled the bill. He was the sun in an age that was all sunshine. ("He was elected largely as a symbol of what Americans admired," is how Samuel Eliot Morison puts it.) But did the boy really know much about him? He knew he had won the war, knew that he was somehow remotely involved with his parents meeting in England, his father an army captain, his mother an army nurse. He knew he had something to do with the army uniforms stored up in the attic—not in trunks yet, not mothballed, but folded fresh across the tops of the trunks. They made for marvelous fun, the times he and his sister dressed up in them. "Eisenhower jackets" they were called. The green-brown fabric, its rich cottony smell, the businesslike buttons, the pockets that still held little flecks of English grass. To him, green GI khaki was the woof and weave of the times. America was the greatest country in the world, and this wasn't just jingoism on his part, but something that was in the air, something those army uniforms exuded, and the boy, inhaling it, was merely being realistic.

When Taffy had her puppies, his parents named the plumpest male "Ike" and the plumpest female "Mamie." All that innocence! And yet in those days, innocence could protect you; it hadn't yet gone flabby or soured. He was startled, shaken even, when one day his father brought home a newspaper with a photo of a subdued, wan-looking Ike in a hospital bathrobe, the slogan JUST FINE, THANKS! embroidered over his heart—his heart that, according to the headlines, had had an "attack," which confused him greatly. Wasn't Ike a general? Wasn't he the one to do the attacking? How could your heart attack you, and did it mean that all the boy loved so much about him and the country and the times and his neighborhood and his family could come crashing down in a flash?

No—or rather, not yet. The newspapers soon showed Ike back at his desk in the Oval Office, and wearing a suit again, not a bathrobe. He ran again in 1956, and the boy was old enough to take an active role in his campaign. All that autumn, when he got home from school, he would don a straw hat, an old-fashioned boater, with a blue I LIKE IKE ribbon wound around the crown, and marched with it up and down the block. He had a campaign button, too, but this was a darker story. It was a huge button, the size of the plates his mother served crustless cream cheese sandwiches on when she had her ladies group over—a button that was meant to be worn right over the heart. It read EISEN-HOWER-NIXON, and had pictures of both of them that shimmered when you tilted the button to the side. Neat—but the boy wouldn't wear it . . . not with that dark, bitter visage glaring out from the right half of the button.

"Why aren't you wearing your button?" his father would ask, but the boy couldn't answer. Because if he loved Ike, then he hated Nixon, with no good reason other than that, when it came to judging faces, his childish intuition was never wrong. Was it because that evil, phony, hateful glare would soon spell doom for everything he loved about his country? He couldn't explain it, so, at his father's prodding, he put the button back on, but lower this time, well down toward his belly, *never* near his heart.

That eight-year-old boy knew nothing of Ike's politics, and if he had, he probably would have approved of them, every child being born a natural conservative, a strong supporter of the establishment status quo. (If he had been the adult he would eventually turn out to be, he would have voted for Stevenson, of course; it was Saul Bellow who said, "Voting for Eisenhower was like casting a vote against the English language.") There must be old people still alive who were born under the rule of history's worst tyrants, were persecuted by them, grew to despise everything they stood for, and yet somewhere in the deepest recesses of their being, when they hear that tyrant's name, can't help smiling in reflexive approbation, simply because that was the name that guided their world when their awareness was at its most impressionable and forgiving.

Ike was no tyrant. What he was (when the boy grew older and began trying to determine whether or not he was indeed worthy of being his first hero) is harder to judge. Certainly, there is much in the poor-boy-from-Abilene-who-grows-up-to-be-president story that is terrifically appealing. What seems to have happened is that while Ike did indeed grow as a man and a leader from those humble beginnings, by the time he became president, he was well past his moral and intellectual prime. ("Good man, wrong business," was House Speaker Sam Rayburn's curt appraisal.) A decent-enough fellow, but decency wasn't enough to overcome that passive Abilene racism he was born with, and decency wasn't enough to destroy Joseph McCarthy before McCarthy destroyed much of the America Ike had pledged to defend. "I won't get down in the gutter with that man," Ike famously growled to his advisors when they urged him to fight back. Under Ike's benevolent smile was a rather small-minded man, at least by this stage.

With Ike you always get the feeling he should have done more—should have gone down to Little Rock in person and taken those black students by the hand, led them past the jeering mob up those high school steps. If he was going to be so good at resembling the Great White Father, then he should have had the courage to act like one, too. Then, too, it's very disillusioning, for someone who vividly remembers being terrified by those duck-and-cover drills in school and all the talk of instant nuclear annihilation, to read that Eisenhower knew very well in 1958 that there wasn't a chance in hell the Russian missiles could have reached us, but that he went ahead and exaggerated the dangers for domestic political reasons. And as for warning us about the military-industrial complex during his famous farewell address—well, thanks, Ike! After you did so much to create it in the first place.

If you read the biographies, there is one place where Eisenhower the hero really comes to life: June 5, 1944, the day before D-Day. The invasion he has charge of has already been postponed once—low cloud cover over France and high winds in the Channel—and now the British meteorologist hands him a forecast that is "iffy" at best. A possible break in the clouds and slightly lower winds, but conditions far from perfect on the 6th. What to do? The moon and tides won't be right for another three weeks, and in the meantime, with a million men in motion on sea and in the air, the chance of the secret leaking out increases each day.

The decision is Ike's alone. Any parent in charge of taking his kids to the beach, any principal trying to decide whether to chance the forecast and have graduation outside, any camp counselor agonizing over whether to climb Mount Baldy in the rain, any fisherman cocking an appraising eye toward thunderheads, knows the complex agony of making weather-based decisions, even on a small scale. It's hard to imagine having to make that decision . . . having to anticipate what the gods would dish out in the next few hours . . . on a scale that was literally the biggest in history.

Ike stares down at the weather report, tries to make sense of the squiggly lines. He looks around at his staff, all of whom suddenly seem to be busy elsewhere. He feels more alone than a boy from Abilene, Kansas, has ever felt—and then, staring into the future, like a hero with classic abilities, he reads that future aright.

"We go," he says—and it's hard in that moment not to like Ike all over again, after all these years. Memory, if stretched far enough, is generously forgiving. When I took my first baby steps of admiration, Ike was the one who held my hand.

DAVE GARROWAY

The boy was there at the birth of television, all right. *There*, as in, he remembered when it wasn't on all day, and if you turned it on in the morning, all you would see were "test patterns" shaped like snowflake crystals. *There*, as in, he remembered when not everyone on the block owned a TV set yet, and neighbors would come over to watch Jackie Gleason on Saturday night. *There*, as in, he remembered the intense heat a TV screen would emit, so you couldn't sit too close, and how there were special lamps you could buy to create "TV light," without which you could easily go blind. He remembered, for that matter, when TV repair was the occupation with the brightest future, and a visit by the TV repairman, with the power to reconnect you, was a big event. "Tube blew on me" was the most frequently repeated phrase of 1953.

One morning he stayed home from school, having come down with what was still referred to as the "grippe." Bored, with nothing better to do, he turned on the Dumont, hoping to find a test pattern he hadn't seen before. Instead, there was a man, an earnest-looking man in glasses, talking very softly and calmly right into the camera. Behind him was a younger man with a warm, friendly smile, and, scampering around his legs, a chimpanzee—a chimp! J. Fred Muggs was his name, because he wore it stenciled on his argyle sweater. Jack Lescoulie turned out to be the name of the smiley-faced one, and Dave Garroway, the man wearing the glasses, was the earnest, sincere one who seemed in overall charge. *Today*, the program was called. The boy instantly felt the rightness of that. *Today*—how beautifully simple!

He called his mother to come and watch with him. (This was the purpose behind having a chimp; it would get kids to watch, and their parents would watch, too.) J. Fred scratched himself with pensive detachment and then jumped up on Jack Lescoulie's lap to give him a hug. Behind a broad desk was a plate-glass window, and people in overcoats and fedoras were staring in, holding up signs with the names of their hometowns. Dave Garroway walked over and smiled at them— and no one in the history of television ever had a softer, nicer smile. Sometimes it seemed like he was smiling just at the boy and no one else—and the boy shyly smiled back.

And the set was open; that was the other thing that fascinated him. You could see the cameramen dollying in for close-ups, the writers hammering away at their typewriters, the makeup women powdering noses and chins. The magic of TV was not hidden here, it was flaunted, and it gave the boy the feeling he was seeing behind all the magician's tricks.

Of the actual show or subsequent shows he remembered only snatches. Grainy film from Korea. Pompous old men being interviewed. The cast from a Broadway musical crowding the set to sing "I Love You a Bushel and a Peck," or "Politics and Poker." Once, a real treat: his favorite puppets, Kukla, Fran, and Ollie. A commercial that they played over and over again—a public service message, with cartoon versions of Benny Goodman, Lionel Hampton, Teddy Wilson, and Gene Krupa playing one of their big hits, and the voice-over explaining how four people from different races could combine to produce some beautiful, swinging harmony—was a radical-enough message for the early 1950s, and a healthy influence on the boy's sympathies.

That this show was *live* was a distinction even a six-year-old understood—it gave what he was watching a believability that the crude film used in, say, *Lassie*, never matched. And as much as he loved J. Fred Muggs and liked Jack Lescoulie, and loved the beautiful "*Today* Girl" (was it Betsy Palmer?), it was Dave Garroway himself he admired most—as unlikely an object of admiration as a boy that age could choose. He would have found this fascination difficult to explain, but it had a lot to do with Garroway's manner. He looked into the screen with a casual kind of earnestness that made it seem he was looking right into your eyes and heart, talking to you and you alone. There was nothing stagy or self-conscious about this; if he had an ego, it was totally hidden. In his manner, there was always "Look at you!" rather than the usual anchorman's "Look at me!" And those glasses! The boy had glasses himself by now, his precocious reading having already taken a toll on his eyes, and to see a man whose glasses seemed even thicker than his own made for a tremendous fellow-feeling right from the start—and fellow-feeling, as it turns out, is one of the key ingredients in admiration.

The TV sets of those years churned out the heat, yet Garroway's face cooled the temperature down. Watching one morning when he was once again home, sick, the entranced boy moved ever closer to the screen, leaned forward, braced himself with his hands on the rug, leaned closer, put his face right up against it, until his glasses touched Garroway's and their partnership was complete.

He always wore bow ties, Garroway did. When the boy went to church that Sunday, he startled his mother by asking to wear a bow tie, too.

The smiling affability, the intellectual flavor, that remarkably compelling earnestness camouflaged a sad-enough story. Garroway's producers, old men now, remember a badly flawed man:

> Garroway was one of the best interviewers who has ever come along . . . It was tragic what happened to him . . . The hours were very difficult. He had to be up at three in the morning. The "Doctor" sustained him and brightened him up, but it also killed him eventually . . . The "Doctor" was liquid codeine. Around two minutes to seven, out would come the little bottle, and he would take a slug. Then the sweep hand would hit seven and he would smile and sparkle and be Dave Garroway until nine o'clock, when he would go back to depressed Dave Garroway . . . As the years went by, he took more and more of it, and it began to befuddle him . . . He said ghosts were menacing him. He said machines had human antagonisms toward him. Sometimes he would grab a microphone in a rage and twist the wire back and forth, muttering, "I'll kill you! I'm strangling you!"

I pretty much forgot about Garroway as I grew up. When my wife and I got married, the first thing we did was throw out our television at the dump. But my early fascination with Garroway, rubbing up against the sad story of what he was like as a man, led me to write a novel called *Morning* based on his career, which came out nearly fifty years from that morning when I'd leaned toward our Dumont TV set to touch eyeglasses. The promise of television in that all-too-brief golden age. The way its potential was squandered, like Garroway's talent was squandered. My own strong connection with those evocative early memories. I turned Garroway into "Alec McGowan," tried my best to capture his characteristic way of looking into a camera:

McGowan stares toward something just to the left of the camera and slightly below it, and then, suddenly, he looks directly into the lens, as if by this quickness to take it unawares, turn it inside out on itself, focus it outwards. He blinks— seems, in the open way he does this, with those feminine eyelashes behind the heavy glasses, the only person who has ever blinked on television before or since—and then squints, the corner of one eye tightening into many wrinkles, the other actually shutting so that he seems like a person who is about to put his eye to a powerful telescope . . . Seeing this, your first reaction is to jump back, and yet immediately afterwards you feel flattered, as if these eyes, out of all possible subjects they might focus on in the enormity of the country, have found your eyes, and your eyes alone, worthy of consideration.

There was a luncheon to kick off the novel, and the organizer did a smart thing: He went to NBC and cadged off them a kineoscope of the first five minutes of the first *Today* show ever, from the autumn of 1952. Magic—thirty seconds into it, and I was a boy again. Many guests had been in television all their lives, and yet they stared at the screen in total silence, as fascinated and enthralled as I was. Garroway, the smoothest of the smooth, is visibly nervous. "We're calling this the *Today* show," he says. "A new way of looking at the world." He leads the camera on a tour of the open set. There, hunched over a desk, typing, puffing away at a cigarette, is Jack Lescoulie. There, behind a large desk, pinned to a bulletin board, are the front pages of that morning's *New York Times* and the *Herald Tribune*. "Here are what we call our Morning Headlines," Garroway says, as the camera dollys in on the newspapers' bold type. It's primitive, naive—and yet, withal, daring and bold.

Charles Osgood was at the luncheon, the veteran CBS newsman who knew Garroway and worshipped him (to the point where, even now, he wears a Garroway bow tie whenever he's on screen). He told me a sad story. The last time he saw Garroway was a few months before he died, when they ran into each other on a Manhattan street corner. Garroway, Osgood said, looked terrific, and seemed just like his old self, full of energy and life, his paranoid demons temporarily banished—but not for long. Osgood had said good-bye and started down the street when he heard Garroway angrily shout his name. He turned and saw Garroway frantically patting the pockets of his suit. "How come you stole my pencil!" he screamed.

"A sad ending," Osgood said, as our elevator touched down. "But you know what? Say this about him. No one—not one of the zillion people who have been on television since—ever related to a camera better than Dave Garroway."

MARY MARTIN

There wasn't much music in the boy's house when he was young. His mother, growing up on a farm in upstate New York during the Depression, never enjoyed frills like music, and it wasn't until late middle age that she completely, out of the blue, developed a passion for Johnny Cash. His father was an even sadder case. As a college boy, he had danced to the music of Benny Goodman and Artie Shaw at road-houses in New Jersey, and he could still foxtrot and jitterbug if the spirit moved him. After the war, though the reason was never clear, he lost most of his eyesight—a handicap he bravely coped with right from the start. Blind people (he was legally blind) often make up for their lack of vision by developing an acute sense of hearing, and come to love music deeply. This would have been a perfect recreation for his father, a passion he could have indulged himself in to the max, but for some reason it never kicked in. Hobby-less, never really comfortable with free time, he would wander around the house on weekends, looking for something or someone to fuss with, humming an old Jimmy Durante ditty all the while—was still humming it sixty years later, without ever once humming anything else.

The boy heard music in church, but it was Sunday school tunes, saccharine and simple, and it wasn't until he was old enough to attend services in the chapel proper that he fell in love with the great old Protestant hymns. In school, it was still kindergarten stuff mostly, songs about sheep, pigs, chickens, and cows.

Not much music—but there was one key exception. Along with their Dumont television set, the boy's parents owned another mirac-ulous fifties invention: a hi-fidelity phonograph with an automatic record changer, one you could pile up to five 33-rpm records on and play each in turn without getting up from the couch. To feed this, they owned some record albums, probably never more than twenty. Some were hardly ever played—Frank Sinatra, Frankie Laine, Julie London—and the ones that did get played were all from Broadway. This was the golden age of the American musical—and, what's more, the boy *knew* it was. Twenty miles to the east, in the great Broadway theaters, *Carousel* was opening, or *Pajama Game,* or *The Music Man* with Robert Preston (which he saw during its first year, as the only boy invited to go along with his sister's Brownie troop). The sheet music and original cast recording would be put on sale the very same week, with almost every song an immediate hit. Even the nonmusical, like his parents, would get swept up in this, shelling out two or three dollars for the album, playing it once or twice, and then pretty much forgetting it was even there.

Their son knew they were there. He must have played them often, worn down their grooves, because years later, when his own kids complained about his being too staid and serious, he would startle them by climbing onto a kitchen chair, throwing his arms apart, and launching into a medley from *My Fair Lady, West Side Story,* or *Fiorello.*

The album he liked best—the one that really got to him, not just in that whistley, finger-snapping spot in the head where good tunes reside, but in the very deepest recesses of his surprisingly ardent young soul—was the original cast recording of *South Pacific.* Listening to this moved him, stirred him, made him cry—almost certainly the very first piece of anything connected to art that did. Ezio Pinza as Emile de Becque, the aging French planter singing about some enchanted evenings. Juanita Hall as Bloody Mary, with her haunting apostrophe to all human yearning, "Bali H'ai." Mary Martin as Nellie Forbush, washing that man right out of her hair. Add to these the boisterous, fun-loving, sex-starved Seabees; the haunting ballad "Younger than Springtime"; the story's brave, ahead-of-its-time treatment of racial prejudice, and the boy was hooked. Starting then, and for the rest of his life, he couldn't hear any of its music, not even a Muzak version in an elevator, without being stirred more deeply and thoroughly than he was by almost any other music.

Why such an extravagant response? He was all of ten years old at the time—but then the secret of ten-year-olds is that they can be furtively, wholeheartedly Romantic. The story reminded him of his own parents' story, how they had met during the war—a story his mother told his sister and he many times. His mother had become a nurse to escape a hard life on the farm, and she'd been the first registered nurse from Syracuse, New York, to volunteer for the army after Pearl Harbor. She was eventually sent to a unit hospital in the rural Wiltshire town of Marlborough, England—a Quonset hut set on the rugby pitch as an operating theater, with drab pyramid tents erected for the nurses to sleep in. It was cold and damp in those tents, and his mother would have done anything to escape. One evening a fellow nurse stuck her head under the wet canvas flap. "There's a lieutenant out here looking for a date; anyone interested?" His mother, just to get warm, volunteered. It was his father, of course. Hardly Emile de Becque, but a handsome, happy-go-lucky kid from Brooklyn.

Close enough. With nurses and war and an "enchanted evening," his parents' story made *South Pacific*'s virtually his own.

No Broadway musical ever had a stronger cast. Ezio Pinza's was once described as "the only human voice acceptable to God." He could pluck beauty and majesty out of the very air, deepening it still further from an overwhelming sense of empathy that could only have come from a tragic sense of life. He had been an opera star before *South Pacific*, famous for his Figaro and Don Giovanni, and listening to him sing "This Nearly Was Mine," the bittersweet anthem to lost love, was probably the first nudge the boy ever had toward becoming an opera fan.

And he had actually seen Juanita Hall in person. She lived in the next town over, and once, while waiting with his parents on the platform of the Long Island Rail Road station, they had nudged him and whispered "Don't look!" It was Juanita Hall, all right, Bloody Mary, with that signature benevolent beam on her betel-nut-colored face—and swathed in mink, if he remembered rightly, so this must have been when she was still performing nightly on Broadway as the toast of the town.

As much as he admired Pinza and Hall, it was nothing compared to how much he loved Mary Martin. The clarity of her voice, where each word was not only enunciated, but celebrated; the all-American fun that was in her tone and phrasing (that signature giggle!); the playful huskiness, the teasing feminine sensuousness, which seemed all-American in a pert, guileless, girl-next-door kind of way; the surprising sadness; her wistfulness without a trace of self-pity. Well, the boy wouldn't have had the words to explain any of this, but what he knew was that every time he heard her voice, he had to stop what he was doing and listen—and that when Mary Martin was done singing, he felt a lot better about things, *any* things, than he had before she began. "A Cockeyed Optimist" was one of the big hits of *South Pacific;* surely Rodgers and Hammerstein had written it just for her.

And sincerity. Who else could sing, in the famous "Twin Soliloquies," a line like "He's a cultured Frenchman / I'm a little hick," without sounding silly? Who else could sing "I'm as corny as Kansas in August," and not make it sound, well, corny? "I expect every one of my chums to make fun / of my proud protestations of love and romance" is the tricky lyric Hammerstein gives her, and the sincere way she puts this over, not letting the forward rhythm of those syllables make her skip across the words' meaning, is the Broadway musical at its highest expression.

Or almost the highest. Wait a bit longer in the song, until the end, with her magic repetition of "I'm in love . . . I'm in love . . . I'm in love . . . I'm in love . . . I'm in love . . . [hesitation] . . . with a wonderful guy!" and listen to what she does with that last word *guy*—and *that's* the American musical at its very summit.

Even the famously dour British critic, Kenneth Tynan, watching her in London, ended up being charmed. "Skipping and roaming around the stage on diminutive flat feet, she poured her voice directly into that funnel into the heart which is sealed off from all but the rarest performers."

For the boy, knowing her first as Nellie Forbush, it was unbearably exciting to see her on television in the famous first live broadcast of *Peter Pan* in 1955. "I'm flying!" she memorably sang, as those all-too-visible ropes (visible? Who cared!) sent her flying high above the NBC soundstage over a majestically campy Cyril Ritchard, swiping malevolently with his sharpened hook.

Still later, the boy must have been one of the very first kids of eventual millions to be marched into a music room, plopped down by a piano, and taught the lyrics to "Do Re Mi," *The Sound of Music* having just opened on Broadway (Martin a bit old for the part, but still a real trouper) singing "My Favorite Things" so exuberantly, with such real joy, it became a standard for the ages from the moment she sang it on opening night.

Am I the last Mary Martin fan left in the world—or at least the last one left under the age of seventy? I suppose. But if your life depended on having a Broadway showstopper sung just right, give me Mary Martin every time.

There's a sequel to my Mary Martin infatuation: As with Garroway, I would one day meet a person who knew her. And not just any person, but James Michener, upon whose *Tales of the South Pacific* the musical was originally based.

He was staying in Woods Hole while attending a meeting of the Oceanographic Institute, of which he was a director. The owner of the motel he stayed in was a pal of mine. My first novel was about to come out, and I was renting a beach shack nearby. Michener and I had the same publisher, and my friend had put all of this together into an invite for me to join the great man for breakfast.

I was shy, deferential; Michener was generously patient and polite. (He looked like a wise and kindly Supreme Court justice, peering down at yet another supplicant.) I couldn't very well admit that I'd never read *Hawaii* or *Centennial* or any of his other famous tomes; what I asked him about was the book I *had* read, hoping it would lead to what it indeed ended up leading to.

"Your *Tales of the South Pacific* was a book I really admired," I told him. He mildly beamed—I don't think he heard many compliments about that one anymore—and then he started talking about when *South Pacific* first opened on Broadway.

As a young author, not quite believing he was part of it all, he would stand in the wings during the performances, watching Pinza and Martin get ready for their roles. Pinza, the handsome old opera star, hardly did any preparation at all; he joked with the stagehands, played poker with his cronies, pinched chorus-girl bottoms as he had been doing for the past thirty years—this, right up to the moment of his cue, when he would go onstage, sing "Some Enchanted Evening," and break everyone's heart.

Martin, on the other hand, was a nervous wreck—no one, according to Michener, ever suffered worse stage fright. She would be sick, she would insist she couldn't do it, this right up to the moment of her cue, when she would prance onstage like a girl without a care in the world, dressed in that baggy sailor suit, singing "Honey Bun" with such playful exuberance that there wouldn't be a single person in the theater who wasn't smiling from ear to ear.

Michener didn't have to draw the moral for me. Professionalism. Grace under pressure. Inner discipline. Both a carefree Pinza and a terrified Martin had it when it counted, and Michener—perhaps meaning to, perhaps not—had given this bashful young writer some valuable advice.

JIM THORPE

Looking back, it's surprising to realize that, though this boy would soon become a passionate reader, his very first heroes came to him largely through what for 1955 was the very latest in high technology: long-playing records and TV. Interesting also that right from the start he was looking for his heroes and role models apart from his family or his immediate surroundings; while he admired his parents, his parents' friends, and his uncles and aunts, he admired them in a take-it-for-granted kind of way that was quite different from what he felt for Dave Garroway or Mary Martin. Again, this may have been because they were too close to him; perhaps a key ingredient of admiration turns out to be that the object has to be at a certain distance, more or less remote. As Montesquieu famously put it, no man is a hero to his butler, and it's something like this that makes admiring your parents not quite the same thing as admiring Dwight David Eisenhower. Call it admiration's Mount Olympus effect—we want our gods, even our lesser gods, way up high and preferably in the mist.

The other surprising thing is that, for the most part, the boy wasn't *taught* to admire, he was left to teach himself. His parents were busy earning a living and running a home, and didn't have any passionate admirations that, by osmosis, could have influenced their son. In Sunday school, he was taught to admire Jesus Christ, but that seemed the only institution motivated by a didactic mission. School tried—Washington's portrait still hung on classroom walls in 1955, and they all made drawings of log cabins on Lincoln's birthday—but in a rather halfhearted way, as if the teachers were already infected with the revisionist mood of the 1960s.

Surprising, too, because teaching by emulation—creating legendary heroes whose lives were so admirable that merely learning of them would make you virtuous—had a long tradition in American education, going all the way back to the infamous Parson Weems tale:

When George Washington was about six years old, he was made the wealthy master of a hatchet, of which, like most little boys, he was immoderately fond and was constantly going about chopping every thing that came his way. "George," said his father, "do you know who killed that beautiful little cherry tree yonder in the garden?" This was a *tough* question, and George staggered under it for a moment, but quickly recovered himself, and looking at his father, with sweet face of youth brightened with the inexpressible charm of all-conquering truth, he bravely cried out, "I can't tell a lie, Pa; you know I can't tell a lie. I did cut it with my hatchet."

"Run to my arms you dearest boy," cried his father in transport. "Run to my arms; glad am I, George, that you killed my tree, for you have paid me back for it a thousand fold. Such an act of heroism in my son is worth more than a thousand trees."

The Parson Weems spirit, ridiculed and (temporarily) abandoned, still managed to live long enough to ensnare the boy in its surprisingly seductive clutches. His restless, compulsive perusal of all the library books he could convince the librarian to let him check out had led him from the farm stories of Walter Brooks (the *Freddy the Pig* books) to a series called *Childhoods of Famous Americans*.

These were short, handsomely printed volumes about the life, particularly the young life, of the usual heroic American suspects, from Benjamin Franklin to Robert E. Lee to Teddy Roosevelt. Many, maybe even most, were devoted to heroes of a somewhat lesser order— Betsy Ross, Eli Whitney, Clara Barton, George Washington Carver, Thomas Edison, Walter Reed. The books would always start with the future hero at home in the little rural town where they inevitably grew up—aged six or seven, with a habit of getting into mischief, whether by staying out too late exploring local caves, or by getting in a fight with the town bully, which his parents, seeing him come home with his face all blooded and his overalls torn, would blame *him* for starting. Similar edifying adventures would occupy all but the final chapter, in which suddenly the boy or girl, with no teenage years to speak of, emerged as a bona fide hero, inventing the cotton gin or the telephone or, in Knute Rockne's case, the forward pass.

By far his favorite book in the series was the one devoted to Jim Thorpe, which he read at least eleven times. The hero portrayed was irresistible: an Indian, a good Sauk and Fox Indian, the kind that got picked on so you could pity him, didn't get mad but quietly went about his business of being excellent, right from his great success at the Carlisle Indian School under his coach Pop Warner, to the point where, winning the decathlon at the 1912 Olympics in Stockholm (last chapter now!), King Gustav V of Sweden, as he draped the gold medal around his neck, said loudly enough so all could hear, "You, Jim Thorpe, are the greatest athlete in the entire world."

That's the old American spirit, all right—sympathy for the underdog, confidence that in the end, those on the bottom will make it to the top. (Which in our times has been turned on its head; we admire the overdog now, believe it fitting that those on top should remain on top; no room on the ladder for upstarts like Thorpe.) To a boy growing up when vestiges of this Horatio Alger spirit lived on, this kind of thing was viscerally compelling—and Jim Thorpe was his favorite precisely because he was the one who out of all these American heroes started from the lowest rung on the ladder.

Looking back, it's obvious that what Childhoods of Famous Americans stoked in the boy was an innate desire for role models he could emulate—for an old-fashioned kind of moral guidance the culture wasn't supplying for him from anywhere else. From the days of Socrates, society has understood not only the value of teaching children to admire, but the deep psychological appetite young people have for learning via such means; ten- and eleven-year-olds don't want to be told that a certain kind of behavior is wrong or right, but if you show them a simple black-and-white morality in action, they find it addictive.

It's easy to make fun of those books, but what they gave the boy, when combined with what he was grabbing from TV and the hi-fi, was a taste for admiration, a liking for the emotion itself, almost regardless of the person who created it in him. His taste would eventually become more discriminating—his golden age of admiration still lay ahead of him—but it's here at the primitive beginning that it's easiest to separate out the various strands that, wound together, make admiring someone one of the deepest pleasures of being human.

Absorbed with himself as all children are, he liked the refreshing self-forgetfulness that came when he was concentrating on a hero— liked to be taken out of himself and transported by the magic of their story. He liked the *frisson* of pleasure that burned a ring around his neck when he heard one of his heroes praised, felt that whenever one of his heroes was being praised, he was being praised, too. He liked the existential reassurance (yes, even then!) that came from knowing that man is good at many difficult and/or beautiful things. Man was a better animal because Jim Thorpe could run so fast, jump so high, throw so far; man was more admirable because Mary Martin could create such beauty with her voice. He liked the Pavlovian response that came with widening name recognition; having received pleasure from admiring someone in the past, then merely the mention of their name would be enough to create that feeling all over again, so there were all these random moments of pleasure available to anyone who stayed alert. This was the "fan club" aspect of admiration, the feeling of belonging to an exclusive fraternity.

And more than this, he liked the fellow-feeling that comes in this early, puppy-love stage of admiration, the sense that if his heroes knew him they would approve of him and be his friend. He liked the feel— this was subtle, but real—that he had to *reach* in order to fully appreciate their talent, had to yearn toward what they offered, and somehow make himself better in order to be fit to admire them in the first place. The feeling, in other words, of betterment, of elevation.

This is what creates childhood admiration, and what can often be its twin, a craving to emulate the heroes and follow in their footsteps. Reading about Ulysses S. Grant and Teddy Roosevelt and Alexander Graham Bell did what it was meant to do—it made him admire them so much that he wanted to be admirable himself. All it took was for him to find a local cave to get lost in, a bully he could stand up to, parents who misunderstood him, a candle he could secretly read by when he was supposed to be sleeping, moral wrongs he could practice righting, right there in his neighborhood, and then one day he would win a place in the pantheon himself.

In the meantime, he had a few heroes under his belt now, a heroine or two besides, and, hitting double digits as far as age went, he was on the lookout for more.

We Are Who We Admire

MICKEY MANTLE

From his earliest years, then, when it came to admiration, two currents carried him along: the eager push from the all-too-obvious suspects, down the river of popular culture; and an alternative side channel carved by the impetus of his own personal imagination, curiosity, rebelliousness, and luck, taking him in another direction entirely. An early bifurcation, the divergent angles of which slowly grew more extreme.

The boy had a distinction he became increasingly proud of the older he became: He was among the very last in the world to ever fall head over heels in love with the old Brooklyn Dodgers. Anyone younger—anyone born later than 1950—would hardly have had any direct personal memory of them, the team having fled Ebbets Field for Los Angeles in 1957. Born in 1948, age seven when they won their first and only World Series, he could remember not only the lovable "Duh Bums," epitomized by the famous sad-faced clown Emmett Kelly (who used to wander sadly around the infield before home games), but how they magically evolved into the legendary "Boys of Summer," a team of consummate, highly skilled professionals, Messrs. Snider, Hodges, Furillo, and Reese.

He remembered the real sadness and dismay when Jackie Robinson . . . Jackie Robinson! . . . was traded to the archrival Giants, and promptly retired. He remembered the tragic January night when Roy Campanella, the great slugging catcher, skidded his car on an icy Brooklyn street and became a paraplegic. He remembered the uproar when the announcement was made that they would be leaving Brooklyn for the West Coast, and, remembering, marveled at how young that makes America seem, to easily recall a time when the thought of having a major league sports team west of St. Louis was a new and radical idea people couldn't quite grasp.

He remembered, most vividly of all, the afternoon his father took him from their home in the suburbs to a game at Ebbets Field. This would have been 1956; the Dodgers, coming off their miraculous 1955 World Championship, were on their way to winning another pennant. His father, Brooklyn-born and -raised, wasn't much of a baseball fan, but he knew the neighborhood, knew how to navigate the trains and subways, and his sure confidence, now that he was back on home turf, made the boy admire him more than usual, even before arriving at the ballpark proper.

The experience—a boy's first major league baseball game with his dad—was everything the myth of baseball would have it be. How urban it all seemed, at least at first—urban in the exposed steel girders and gridwork of the actual stadium, the unapologetic concrete of the concourses and ramps, the rich urban fumes, and the hip-hoppity, piebald pigeons. And how, in a magic transformation he would never quite get over, this suddenly opened—as he and his father climbed the last ramp and turned left toward their seats—into a brilliant bright swath of absolute rural beauty, with the startling green grass of the outfield, the rich brown earth of the base paths, the players, in their baggy white uniforms, shagging pregame flies like soft-mouthed cows catching apples.

That's for starters. Add on to these the malty beer smell (he knew it was beer, from his father's Friday night poker parties, but the smell was still new and exotic to him), the raucous cacophony of the fans who were every bit as rabid as legend has it, and the excitement of the game itself, with Don Newcomb pitching against the soon-to-be-great Milwaukee Braves, with Messrs. Mathews, Adcock, and Aaron. How two men just behind them, within touching distance, paraded around a banner reading WIN OR LOSE, WE LOVE OUR DODGERS!, and how right behind them marched the "Dodger Symphony," beating out a terrific rhythm on washboards, whistles, pots, and pans. And while he remembered how that outfield expanse first hit him, he could also remember how small Ebbets Field was, so you looked right down on the players below—could wave to your favorites with every expectation that they could see you and wave back. And the billboards on the outfield walls—were they really for products called Burma Shave and Bosco and Brylcreem, or was that a nostalgic part of his memory pasting them there instead?

What boy could resist it? All the greater, then, his confusion and sadness when the Dodgers left for California, taking with them not only his first and most short-lived of team allegiances, but also his earliest heroes who were black.

This left a vacuum—any male his age, growing up in the greater New York metropolitan area between 1957 and 1962 can tell you about the vacuum this left in a young fan's heart—into which rushed the only professional baseball team left in the city, and its greatest star.

He would live long enough to become mildly embarrassed by this, his boyhood infatuation with the New York Yankees and Mickey Mantle. It's a terrible thing for a novelist to admit, that he once identified with the sports equivalent of General Motors. How much more fitting it would be to talk of his lifelong love affair with the Chicago Cubs of Ernie Banks, or, better still, his raging passion for the Kansas City Athletics and Bob Cerv. But no, when it came to forming allegiances, he was strictly local. And local, between the time the Dodgers and Giants left town in 1957 and the Mets arrived in 1962, meant rooting for the Yanks.

As for Mantle, much has been written about him in much the same vein. An incredibly raw talent from the boonies makes it big in New York, suffers crippling injuries, soldiers on in brilliant fashion—the white guy who suburban kids all over the country identified with, the one whose cards, if your mom didn't toss them out and you didn't put rubber bands around them, can now put your kid through two years of college. Mickey Mantle, who through the fifties and early sixties was the sexy male equivalent of Marilyn Monroe.

Mantle's legend, like Monroe's myth, was largely a construct of the publicity people and the papers, but, as with Monroe, there was a great deal in Mantle that was sheer organic talent. That's what the boy fell for, why he collected Mantle cards and copied his stance in Little League (feet closed, shoulder turned and slightly dipped, bat held vertically back by the hip). He loved the tape-measure shots, loved the manly/boyish aw-shucks beauty of his face—and when he turned out to be a badly flawed hero, when his knees started to go, he only loved him all the more.

For Mantle, as cliché-ridden as his reputation soon became, at least put courage out on the table as a virtue worth emulating—and who else could you say this about in 1959? Not explorers, for there weren't any (well, one, but we'll talk about him later). Not generals, for we weren't involved in a shooting war. Not civil rights heroes, though they would soon make a difference. The culture had a courage vacuum. Athletes had to take up the slack, not only here, but with virtues of many kinds, and Mantle was for a decade the epitome of physical courage, the exemplar of toughing it out. He hit a lot of homers, but it was those bloody bandages that came off his legs after every game that made him Homeric.

"Come on, my friends," the host says when Odysseus lands on Phaeacia's shores. "Let us ask our guest over there what game / he's good in; He's built like a man indeed, what with / Those legs and arms and that powerful neck of his; / He's bound to be strong, and surely he's still young enough / Though broken by many misfortunes."

I saw him play at least five times, judging by the scorecards I've saved, but I only retain two vivid memories. One was from a game in 1963, when he was still very much in his prime—an afternoon game against the old Washington Senators, where Pedro Ramos tossed a ball too close to Clete Boyer's head, and manager Ralph Houk, the tough old World War II vet, stormed out of the dugout and kicked at home plate so viciously that the entire infield was enveloped by the resulting red cloud. Mantle—the memory that sticks—walked. As always when he drew a walk, he chatted easily with the opposing first baseman— even from our seats behind the third-base dugout, I could catch that trademark self-deprecating boyish smile. Somehow he made it to second base, a fielder's choice probably, and now the stage was set for the drama that bound me to his side nearly forever.

For Mantle, having made it with no sweat to second, now decided to steal third base. Famous for being a big man with speed, he didn't run much anymore; he needed to protect those pins. But now he ran—and I was late picking up on it. I'd turned to watch the pitch, and it was a sudden, startled, sheep-like bleat, combined with a glimpse of heads snapping quickly to the left, that alerted me as to what was up. Our seats behind third base were *right* behind third, so Mantle, in his desperation to beat the throw, ran directly for us—directly for *me*. I recognized instantly the pain on his face—his tongue hanging out, his eyes winced backwards, every feature distorted and smeared by effort. He ran like a locomotive, not a gazelle—you could all but see the steam puffs trailing off his shoulders—so the effect wasn't of speed but of power. The catcher—I had totally forgotten the catcher—had let loose his peg, and now Mantle was sliding, throwing his arms up, so his face was even more distorted—this really hurt! The ball arrived with a plop we could plainly hear; third-base coach Frank Crosetti screamed like a seagull and cursed; the umpire peered down into this newest red cloud, then jerked his hand up. Mantle, with probably the most empty, vapid, emotionless look I'd ever seen on a man's face, trotted back to the dugout—out—out by a country mile, but more my hero than ever.

Marianne Moore wrote a poem called "The Hero" that describes what I saw in the Mantle of those years, that lonely, faraway look in his eyes, as if he was really meant to be a hardscrabble farmer in Oklahoma after all, and the rest had all been a dream. "Suffering and not saying so; standing and listening where something was hiding . . . tired but hopeful— / hope not being hope / until all ground for hope has vanished."

Hope vanished quickly for Mantle and his fans. By '65, the Yanks were about to enter their decade-long Dark Ages as strictly a second-division club—a decline largely caused by their racist failure to sign any black stars. Mantle's legs were a joke now, and his was clearly a case of someone hanging on too pathetically long. They threw a valedictory "Mickey Mantle Day" for him on September 18, 1965, and I was there, though I don't remember much except how we all stood on our feet every time he came up, hoping beyond hope for a home run that never came. The Detroit pitcher (was it Denny McLain?) stole the show with a generous gesture; when Mantle first came up, McLain walked in from the pitcher's mound and shook his hand.

I still have a program from that day; it's beside me on the desk as I write. There's a nice oil painting of the Mick on the cover, which the caption explains is a "Cover illustration from Mickey Mantle's *The Quality of Courage*, published by Bantam Books, available wherever paperbacks are sold," and it reminds me how "courage" had become so closely linked with Mantle that it had now become a marketable commodity. The copy inside the program underlines the point. "His awesome power, his determination to play despite a heartbreaking series of injuries, his speed afoot, his switch-hitting prowess, and the overall dramatics of his performance have made Mickey Charles Mantle one of the game's most spectacular performers."

Let it go at that. Let it go . . . But too many men my age can't let it go, and have spent the rest of their lives pining nostalgically for a Mantle that probably never existed. Mantle taught me that some admirations have to be brutally dropped. His lame years when he played a bad imitation of himself, the stories that came out in a franker age of his womanizing and boozing and meanness, the sleazy last act when, an alcoholic, he jumped ahead of the queue to get a liver transplant. There was nothing admirable in any of this, and I only felt a flicker of wistful sadness when the end finally came.

DAVY CROCKETT

The thing you have to remember about crazes, whether they were for hula hoops or The Beatles, is that they happen to one person at a time, times many millions. Almost every white boy in America fell for Davy Crockett simultaneously, but the young boy we're focusing on here was hardly aware of any of them. Watching Crockett on TV, he watched him alone, and was always surprised to learn that any of his friends watched, too, so personal was the Crockett-Wetherell relationship. For Davy struck him right in the heart, the perfect hero at the perfect time. Quietly strong, dryly humorous, handsome, manly, modest—and all of these things out in the woods!

Whether by luck or by calculation, Disney had done something very shrewd with their new Crockett series. Instead of yanking out a hero from the already-timeworn myth of cowboys and Indians, they had gone back to an earlier era, tapping into the even richer tradition of Daniel Boone, Natty Bumppo, and George Rogers Clark. This turned out to be the key to the Crockett craze—romanticizing an era when the frontier was closer at hand, just west of the Appalachians. Unlike cowboys babysitting heifers, these were men who had their families in tow, who split logs in virgin forest, who faced real danger, not the trouble that came in bars.

It had been 130 years since this world had existed, but the cultural residue ran deep enough that it tapped into the long American romance with a wild, unfettered land. "For a transitory enchanted moment, man must have held his breath in the presence of this continent," Fitzgerald famously wrote—but he was wrong about how long that moment lasted. Put it at roughly 350 years, from the time Gosnold sailed along the New England coast, to a time, in the bland 1950s suburb the boy grew up in, when he and his pals could still find escape and adventure prowling the local vacant lot, coonskin caps over their heads, fringed buckskin on their jackets, long Kentucky rifles held ready at their sides, pretending they were Davy Crockett or his wisecracking buddy, Georgie Russell. Playing cowboy, you shot at things just for the hell of it; playing Crockett, you shot at things that shot at you first.

The shows themselves (were there ever more than five or six of them?) were of a very high standard. Fess Parker (Fess!) was the personification of modest manly courage, and, what's rarer, he seemed to be a philosophizer, a serious thinker, someone who had real depth. Buddy Ebsen was hilarious as his sidekick—a comedian who had a serious, tender side, too. Throw in a boisterous Mike Fink, a dignified but amoral Andy Jackson, Jim Bowie with his famous knife, set them all down on the Mississippi or the Kentucky hills or the Alamo, and what red-blooded ten-year-old American boy wouldn't be entranced? And Crockett really existed, too, back in history—we were falling for a fictional nonfictional character, a confusion we'd all have more experience with later.

There was a sordid side to the Crockett craze, it being the TV series that introduced mass merchandise that was really *mass* merchandise, possessing an irresistible appeal. The Crockett coonskin cap with the dangling tail was his famous symbol, of course, but there were also Crockett jackets, Crockett pants, Crockett "Betsy" rifles, Crockett lampshades, comic books, ViewMaster slides, and everything else the

Disney marketers could think of. It would be nice to think that the boy was immune to all this, that his love for Crockett was on a loftier plane, but no, he never wanted anything so much as that first Crockett cap, was never so disappointed as when he discovered, plopping it over his crew-cut red hair, that it didn't fit.

A blow—but his fascination with Crockett only grew more intense. In the next-to-last episode, Crockett and Russell gallop off toward the Alamo to help defend the beleaguered garrison. What fascinated him most was the moral dimension Crockett had. *Be sure you're right, then go ahead* was his motto, repeated in several key scenes, and to the boy, whose only moral precepts at the time came from Sunday school, this seemed like Schopenhauer. *Be sure you're right, then go ahead.* The second he apprehended what this meant, it became his motto, too. How simple! How brave! How clear!

Or not. For even an eleven-year-old could sense the weak point here—how did you *know* when you were right? As an ethical rule, it was a bit shaky, though the U.S. was about to give it a real workout in Vietnam. So, the boy, luckily for his moral health, saw through it just in time. At least, as with Mantle and courage, it put morality out on the table as something to consider, and this, plus the romance of the outdoor life, were the two Crockett influences that made a real and lasting impact.

As for Crockett himself, what I've read of him makes him even more appealing than the Disney version—a self-promoting (in a proto–Muhammad Ali vein), tall-tale teller, whose writing style presages Mark Twain's. Here's that long-forgotten literary historian, Van Wyck Brooks (a critic I admired), explaining the real Crockett's unique flavor and the role he plays in American mythology:

> Among these men who were living legends, half hidden
> by their forest lives, David Crockett was perhaps the most
> renowned, a mighty hunter and a storyteller beyond compare
> in his great garden of Tennessee . . . He moved from clearing
> to clearing and from cabin to cabin, for he wished his boys
> to grow up in ever wilder country, where the varmints were
> always more dangerous and better sport. There his dogs

Whirlwind, Soundwell and Growler, Holdfast, Deathmaul and Grim could show that they were worthy of Betsy, his rifle . . . People were in the habit of saying, when anything out of the way occurred, "Just the same, I can tell you it's nothing to Crockett" . . . Like the Western tales, these monstrous fictions were allied to the physical features of the country, the stupendous mountains, the vast rivers, plains that were boundlessly fertile and animals of wondrous variety, fierceness and size.

Sir Edmund Hillary

One of the boy's earliest television memories was the coronation of Queen Elizabeth in June of 1953, when he wasn't quite five years old. His mother was excited about it, the whole adult world was excited, and somehow this excitement was communicated to him. He'd heard enough fairy tales to know a queen was a very big deal, even if he understood that this one wasn't quite ours. That she had the same name as his mother only added to her majesty; when the archbishop man lowered the crown on her small, feminine, very fragile-looking forehead, he was watching with the kind of intentness that burns memory in deep. He remembered all the pomp, which went right to that ardent royalist spot every small child has in their heart; he remembered Prince Philip, with all those ribbons and braid; he remembered Sir Winston Churchill, who the camera kept coming back to, especially since he always seemed to be wiping away tears.

There's a memory not quite vivid enough for specific detail which is attached to all this. The day before the coronation, word had reached London that the team of British climbers led by Sir John Hunt had succeeded in climbing Mount Everest for the first time—a feat that, coupled with the coronation, seemed to breathe life back into the British spirit after the beating it had taken during the war. Surely the commentators were talking about this while the boy watched the coronation, because it seemed in later years that he had witnessed the climb "live," too, though clearly that's impossible. In 2003, when the fiftieth anniversary was celebrated—both of Queen Elizabeth's reign and the conquest of Mount Everest—he felt as strong a shot of nostalgia as if he had been a participant in both.

He always had a soft spot in his heart for Queen Elizabeth, and nestled right beside it was a sterner admiration for Sir Edmund Hillary and his partner on the summit, the Sherpa, Tenzing Norgay. The lean, fit Hillary photographed lounging on a scree slope as the party begins its climb, is a tremendously appealing male figure, with a strong aquiline face, a quietly cocky New Zealand smile that bad teeth make all the more magnetic, and—for the boy, the absolute crowning touch—a foreign legionnaire's hat that he always wore, with a striped linen flap hanging over his neck to protect it from the sun.

Hillary was certainly the last man to achieve widespread fame as an explorer, so even a boy growing up in the pancake-flat suburbs could idolize him, dream of conquering mountains himself. What's more, he didn't just look like a hero—he really was one. James Morris, a writer of exceptional talent, was a member of Hunt's expedition, covering it for the *London Times*. Years later, having had a sex change operation, he became Jan Morris, and wrote even more brilliantly. Here's his take on the Hillary of 1953:

> Hillary worked in the half-light, huge and cheerful, his movement not so much graceful as unshakably assured, his energy almost demonic. He had a tremendous bursting, elemental, infectious, glorious vitality about him, like some bright burly diesel express pounding across America; but beneath the good fellowship and the energy, there was a subtle underlying seriousness; he reminded me often of a musician in the hours before a concert, when the nagging signs of nervous tension are beginning to enter his conversation, and you feel that his pleasantries are only a kindly facade. Hillary was as much a virtuoso as any Menuhin, and as deeply and constantly embroiled in his art; I first detected signs of greatness in him that evening below Camp III, as the ice chips flew through the darkness, his striped hat bobbed in the chasm. . . .

Everest had been a splendid team effort, but that only enhanced Hillary's achievement. He had gone where no man had ever gone before, and it wasn't a cliché, but a real extension of human capabilities. The boy read Sir John Hunt's *The Conquest of Everest* again and again, especially the part where Hunt puts down his pen and lets Hillary tell the story of that final summit bid:

> As I chipped steps around still another corner, I wondered rather dully just how long we could keep it up. Our original zest had now quite gone and it was turning more into a grim struggle. I then realized that the ridge ahead, instead of still monotonously rising, now dropped sharply away, and far below I could see the North Col and the Rongbuk Glacier. I looked upward to see a narrow snow ridge running up to a snowy summit. A few more whacks of the ice ax in the firm snow and we stood on top . . . I looked at Tenzing and in spite of the balaclava, goggles and oxygen mask, all encrusted with long icicles that concealed his face, there was no disguising his infectious grin of pure delight as he looked all around him. We shook hands and then Tenzing threw his arms around my shoulders and we thumped each other on the back until we were almost breathless.

After Everest, Hillary led the first expedition to cross the Antarctic continent, and thanks to getting *National Geographic,* the boy was able to follow every frozen step of the way. Hillary was then signed up by Sears, Roebuck & Co. to be their official "advisor" on their outdoor gear, so every sleeping bag for summer camp you bought at Sears, every folding cot, every kerosene lantern, had EDMUND HILLARY scrawled on the side, and the boy was sufficiently a purist to find this cheesy, even degrading. The image he had of Sir Edmund was of someone standing alone on a cold mountain summit, lofty, above it all, not someone whose stuff you could buy from flabby-looking clerks at your local Sears. Like Mantle, like Crockett, his heroism was used to sell things; the boy, as well as getting lessons in admiration, was learning very quickly how contemporary capitalism sucked you in.

Hillary was the first mountain climber whose exploits I followed with real fascination, though there would be others, including Lionel Terray, the famous French climber who was a hero on so many peaks, and Maurice Herzog, who wrote the classic, *Annapurna*. Not content with armchair mountaineering, I eventually took a crack at learning how to climb—an attempt that ended ironically and sadly, when I broke both my arms in the Bugaboo Mountains of British Columbia when I was twenty-two. A long story, which isn't nearly as dramatic as I've just made it sound. Suffice it to say, I ventured far enough into mountaineering to know I didn't have the stamina or the very specialized aptitude it calls for. The fuel of admiration can often pump the motor of emulation, but it's important to accept the fact that the emulation can often fizzle and stall.

Nevertheless, Hillary is someone I still admire. He spent much of his active life going back again and again to the Himalayas, building schools for the Sherpas, seeing that they were treated fairly by the climbing expeditions that hired them, bettering their lot, to the point where he achieved something like sainthood among the people he loved best. And if that wasn't enough to preserve my admiration, there's that autograph I mentioned in the introduction to this book, the one he sent to my son. *Ed Hillary,* it reads—very simple, nothing else—but combined with the New Zealand stamp on the letter, my son's name and address obviously written by the great old man himself, it made me decide that if ever in a sour, disillusioned mood I begin kicking heroes out of my personal pantheon, the last person to go will be Sir Edmund Hillary.

T. H. WHITE

Heroism and courage—it's what the boy was interested in during those years—so it's not surprising that his quest to learn more about both subjects led him to *The Once and Future King* by British author T. H. White, the modern (well, circa 1940) updating of Malory's King Arthur epics. It's a book that's always been in print, though the various Tolkien crazes have tended to overshadow White's equally substantial achievement. Like many classic children's books, it's not really for children at all, unless they are precocious readers and/or interested in explicit discussions of heroism and fate. It's a postmodern novel before there was postmodernism—part epic, part commentary on that epic, a novel that doesn't take itself too seriously, and, by this very lightness, ends up being very serious indeed. It's much more readable than Tolkien—White was smart enough not to try and write in a mock-medieval prose style—and much more humorous. After reading the first exuberant paragraph, the boy was totally hooked:

On Mondays, Wednesdays and Fridays it was Court Hand and Summulate Logicales, while the rest of the week it was the Orangon, Repetition and Astrology. The governess was always getting muddled with her astrolabe, and when she got specially muddled she would take it out on the Wart by rapping his knuckles. She did not rap Kay's knuckles, because when Kay grew older he would be Sir Kay, the master of the estate. The Wart was called the Wart because it more or less rhymed with Art, which was short for his real name. Kay had given him the nickname. Kay was not called anything but Kay, as he was too dignified to have a nickname and would have flown into a passion if anybody had tried to give him one. The governess had red hair and some mysterious wound from which she derived a lot of prestige by showing it to all the women of the castle, behind closed doors. It was believed to be where she sat down, and to have been caused by sitting on some armor at a picnic. Eventually she offered to show it to Sir Ector, who was Kay's father, had hysterics and was sent away.

The Wart, the young King Arthur, is transformed by his tutor Merlin into various animals, and learns lessons about the world from the convincingly rendered point of view of ants, fish, or birds (these are among the best passages, White being a self-taught naturalist of real insight). Here, for example, the Wart, temporarily a wild, white-fronted goose, has his pretensions punctured by a friendly, albeit sarcastic, gander:

"My name is Ly-lyok," she said. "You had better call your-self Kee-Kwa, and then the rest will think you came from Hungary."

"Do you all come here from different places?"

"Well, in parties of course. There are some here from Siberia, some from Lapland, and I can see one or two from Iceland."

"But don't they fight each other for pasture?"

"Dear me, you are a silly," she said. "There are no bound-aries among the geese."

"What are boundaries, please?"

"Imaginary lines on the earth, I suppose. How can you have boundaries if you fly? Those ants of yours—and the humans, too—would have to stop fighting if in the end they took to the air."

"I like fighting," said the Wart. "It's knightly."

"Because you are a baby."

It's White's willingness to be very explicit about heroism and courage and the ways of the world that fascinated the boy, though the characterization was superb as well. Merlin—who in White's telling is a cross between Groucho Marx and Gandalf—is always getting his spells mixed up and confusing the future with the past, but he's always wise when the kingdom's fate is on the line and his advice counts. King Arthur, the grown-up Wart, is thoughtful, sensitive—a reluctant king, who yearns to use his power for good, and is always stumbling over power's contradictions. Lancelot, the bravest of the Round Table, is a knight for our times, an anti-knight, and the fact that he's convinced he's ugly made the boy, with his buckteeth and pimples, identify with him very closely:

The boy thought there was something wrong with him. All through his life—even when he was a great man with the world at his feet—he was to feel this gap: something at the bottom of his heart of which he was aware and ashamed, but which he did not understand . . . He had already decided that when he was a grown knight he would give himself a melancholy title. He was the oldest son, he was bound to be knighted, but would not call himself Sir Lancelot. He would call himself the Chevalier Mal Fet—the Ill-Made Knight.

Guinevere? Well, there's no one harder to write about than a bona fide princess, but White portrays her as a very believable young girl always a bit bewildered at the prominence life has brought her. Here, Lancelot has been trying to teach her falconry, and he's become angry at her clumsiness:

> The young man knew, in this moment, that he had hurt a real person, of his own age. He saw in her eyes that she thought he was hateful, and that he had surprised her badly. She had been giving kindness, and he had returned it with unkindness. But the main thing was that she was a real person. She was not a minx, not deceitful, not designing and heartless. She was pretty Jenny, who could think and feel.

The other intriguing thing about White's book is that you learn a lot reading it—its feel of arcana on chivalry, falconry, and medieval armor and fighting. White—who led a very sad life himself—once wrote: "The best thing for being sad is to learn something," and he obviously was an author who took his own advice.

The boy took in these Arthurian heroes differently than he did those heroes who came to him served on the plate of TV. If he had been asked about this, he might have pondered for a while, grimaced, struggled to find the correct words to explain what he meant. On television, even in newspapers, heroes seemed real to him, but the heroes he met while reading fiction, though "made up," seemed real-er. Real-er—it's the neologism he would finally have come to. For all that he admired Mickey Mantle, the one and only time he ever managed to penetrate the baseball player's aura was the time he'd steamed toward him behind third base, his face contorted in effort, his tongue all but hanging out. With Lancelot, Arthur, and Guinevere, he felt he was inside their hearts all the time; there was real magic afoot in White's novel, White being every bit as good a sorcerer as Merlin. Fiction—and he would have to think a lot more about this in his life—was the medium heroes grew best in. Then, too, though he wouldn't have had words yet for this either, he was shrewd enough, even at eleven, to understand that questions of ethics, of power, of how to conduct yourself in the world toward those you loved, were a lot more important than worrying about batting averages and standings, a lesson many of his contemporaries, clinging to their childhoods, never quite learned.

I suppose T. H. White himself is largely forgotten now, but he's a writer worth going back to, and not just for *The Once and Future King*. His *Mistress Masham's Repose* is a classic children's novel, written from the perspective of a wise and witty adult who still retains a child's sense of wonder. *The Goshawk*, his nonfiction account of coming to terms with a willful, intelligent goshawk, is the best falconry book ever written, and a minor classic in the vast genre of human-animal understanding.

He had a bittersweet life, White did; he was what in that era was called a "latent" homosexual, which meant he was too guilty and ashamed to ever find a companion who might have eased his loneliness ("The boy thought there was something wrong with him . . . something at the bottom of his heart of which he was aware and ashamed, but which he did not understand"). To smother the hurt, he became an expert hunter, fly fisher, and falconer, and lived in the most remote areas of rural Britain where his avocations were right at hand.

Julie Andrews, the Broadway star, came to know him well. "Tim had huge mood swings. On a good day, he was the best companion you could ever ask for. Anything you wanted to know, Tim was the one to tell you. He knew everything about the universe: the stars, nature, fishing, sailing, geology, history. He *was* Merlin: wise, thoughtful, caring, dear. But when he was drunk, it was best to leave him alone."

Then, very late in his life, a curious thing happened. He became famous overnight. Lerner and Loewe, fresh off their triumph with *My Fair Lady*, distilled the essence of White's story into their musical, *Camelot*, which was one of the last Broadway hits in the old style, where nearly every song was an immediate hit. Commentators, enchanted by the new president and his wife, immediately began calling the Kennedy White House "Camelot," which, if they had gone back to White's version, they might have realized wasn't quite the sunny, idyllic appellation they thought it was. Even a smart, shrewd historian like Samuel Eliot Morison fell for this; he concludes his majestic *The Oxford History of the American People* (which my father gave me for getting good grades my junior year in high school) by quoting a verse from the musical to sum up the feeling of loss at Kennedy's death:

> Ask ev-ry person if he's heard the stor-y
> And tell it strong and clear if he has not;
> That once there was a fleet-ing wisp of glory
> Called Cam-e-lot . . . Don't let it be for-
> Got . . . That once there was a spot
> For one brief shin-ing
> Mo-ment . . . That was known as Cam-e-lot.

Lost in Admiration

WALT KELLY

A boy who set out to worship only "heroes" could have starved to death in the early '60s, unless he swallowed the obvious candidates the culture had on offer. There was Tom Dooley—not the sad figure of the Kingston Trio's famous hit, but a missionary of the muscular Christian sort, who for a short period was held up by the media as an American version of Albert Schweitzer. Laos was his mission's focus, unluckily for Dooley, who, after writing a couple of best-sellers, died of cancer, and had his work forgotten in the tidal wave of evil that crashed upon that part of the world. There was, to compare cultural extremes, Elvis Presley, who had been discharged from the army and was trying to pick up his career where he had left off, but sadly, he was addicted to cheeseburgers.

The boy, entering his teens, had no use for Presley, and neither did his friends; worship of Elvis marked and continues to mark a real generational divide, with people slightly older idolizing him, making him their King, while baby boomers mostly thought he was ridiculous with the pelvis stuff, and those gyrations.

There was a much closer call with the original astronauts, the *Mercury* Seven. These were to be the last "hero" heroes that the establishment tried hard to have everyone worship—heroes of the old sort, military men and pilots, stalwart, laconic, clean . . . the last "Right Stuff" before the publicity mills began specializing in sports stars and celebrities. Tom Wolfe would eventually make mincemeat of the "Seven" in his debunking best-seller, but that was fifteen years in the future, and the boy didn't need to be debunked of them, because he never quite swallowed the company line on them anyway. Yes, he was one of those who was herded into his junior high school auditorium to watch the latest *Mercury* blastoff from Cape Canaveral; yes, he knew all their names, knew what their wives and kids looked like, had his own personal favorite (Wally Schirra, the boyish-looking one), but, emotionally, he never bought into their heroism; he thought them plucky, but not much more.

This seems to have been a fairly typical reaction to the astronauts—that there was a kind of generalized admiration for them right through the moon landings, but a remote sort of admiration, since, let's face it, they didn't seem heroic when they were being human, and they didn't seem human when they were being heroic. Lounging at home with their families as the *Life* photo crew snapped pictures, tossing a football around on their lawns pre-mission, they were as human as the family next door, but that was part of their problem. Suited up, strapped to their life support, they didn't look human at all, even with the vigorous thumbs-ups they would give the cameras before disappearing through the fretwork of the gantry into their capsules—they looked like the Michelin tire man.

The one bona fide hero of those years, Martin Luther King, Jr., did not immediately make an impact on the boy. The media—at least the media that reached the boy's house—had not yet made up its mind about King. He was still more of a rabble-rouser, a troublemaker, than he was a saint. The civil rights movement had certainly caught his attention, though, pricked his conscience, raised his consciousness. He read about the boys and girls not much older than himself who sat in at the segregated lunch counters in North Carolina, and had ketchup poured over their heads by a mob who stood behind their stools, jeering. This he could relate to, all right. These were the days when the W. T. Grant stores still dominated American downtowns, including his, and the Grant's lunch counter was the equivalent (no, not the equivalent, but so much more) of today's McDonald's. He could picture himself sitting there while people yelled and screamed in his ear, perhaps about his being a redhead (his one conspicuous vulnerability), and, imagining this, he knew that he himself could never summon up the heroism displayed by those lunch-counter demonstrators.

King would have to wait a few years before seizing the boy's imagination. The astronauts were definitely out. Kennedy never spoke to him. What seemed to be happening was that his admiration was becoming a bit more discriminating, a bit more selfish, less likely to listen to what the world at large was telling him. Maturing, in other words—that dreaded word adults were all too likely to hurl at you as a taunt. He didn't need heroes just to satisfy a generalized craving anymore; what he was looking for were admirations that were a little out of the mainstream, ones that could help shape him, influence him, make him what he struggled incoherently to be. Antiheroes might be the label for the next bunch, but they weren't quite that. They were *of* the establishment—otherwise, he wouldn't have learned about them—but they poked fun at it, mocked it, turned it on its head—and this is exactly the note a fourteen-year-old looks for, with that jaded, ironical, skeptical worldview that really isn't jaded, ironic, or skeptical at all.

Newsday, his local paper, had a fine comics page. There were plenty of superheroes, but they seemed exaggerated and over-the-top to him, and even the terrestrial heroes like Dick Tracy and Brenda Starr failed to capture his imagination, while Li'l Abner seemed to him mostly mean. He remembered enjoying Donald Duck, to an embarrassingly ripe old age, but then DD was always Disney's most antiestablishment creature, and the strip included the wonderfully miserly Uncle Scrooge. *Pogo* he was certainly aware of—*Newsday* always printed it on the top left, in a position of honor—but for a long time he was repelled by its densely textured artwork, its experiments with font, its balloons spilling toward the edges, the innovations that made it hard to read unless you were willing to make an effort—and who expected comics to require effort? It was set in the Okefenokee swamp, and yes, there was something impenetrable and swamp-like about it at first glance, and the boy just wasn't interested in pushing through the vines and moss to see what was going on inside the swamp's secret heart.

And then, between one afternoon and the next, he was interested, passionately interested; he became a *Pogo* freak, and for that matter, forty years later, he still was. The key was one day stumbling upon one of the compilations, the books, they would put together from time to time, perhaps *I Go Pogo,* which, bent, battered, and smelling vaguely of bananas, still retains an honored spot on his shelves. *Pogo* had a narrative complexity that was better served in the longer Sunday strips than it was in the daily ones, and was better served by books than it was by Sundays, Walt Kelly being a graphic novelist, though no one in that era would have been pretentious enough to call him that.

The other secret about *Pogo* was that it wasn't for kids at all, so falling in love with it marked a real advance in his journey toward adulthood. The animals lured the kid part of him into the swamp, but it was the satire and humor that held him there—and the world's best satire has always come to us via animals. Driving to the family summer home by a lake in Connecticut, ensconced in the backseat with *Potluck Pogo* or *The Incompleat Pogo*, he would startle his parents by suddenly laughing out loud. Albert the Alligator was involved in a "thinking contest" with Houn'dog, and, after some preliminary skirmishing, they ratchet up the pace:

> Albert: I is thinkin' of grass . . . ALL THE GRASS BLADES IN THE WORLD!
>
> Houn'dog: I is thinkin' of SAND. ALL THE SAND GRAINS ANYWHERE!
>
> Albert: I is thinkin' of String upon String of HOT DOGS an' . . . an' . . . an' . . .
>
> Houn'dog: I is thinkin' of POPCORN . . . All what's already popped . . . an' all what's poppin' NOW. POP. POP. POP. POP.
>
> Albert: If he gonna run up a big score by jes' MENTAL POPPIN' corn an' countin' each pop . . . I'se gonna think of SPRING FROGS PEEPIN' THEIR LIL' HEARTS OUT IN THE APRIL EVE . . . *peep peep peep peep* . . .
>
> Houn'dog: Pop pop pop pop . . .
>
> Albert: Peep peep PEEP PEEP . . .

His parents, bless their mystified hearts, pretended to laugh along with him.

Pogo, even during its heyday in the 1950s and early '60s, was never to everyone's taste. It seems, on first glance, so much more crowded than a normal cartoon, so much more complicated. No other strip ever played around more with language and puns; no other strip ever used balloons so imaginatively, or contained so many creative misspellings or experimented so wildly with font. (P. T. Bridgeport, the impresario bear, talks in circus-poster type; Deacon, the sanctimonious muskrat, talks in Gothic script.) It was the most literary of comic strips, and the wordplay is merged with absolutely original and richly detailed art. Cross James Joyce with Goya, throw in some Lewis Carroll, turn the resulting creature into a cartoonist, and you would end up with Walt Kelly.

Most of all, remembering *Pogo*, you remember the marvelous characters. Churchy LaFemme, the turtle poet. Porky Porcupine, the sourpuss with the heart of gold. Albert Alligator, the boy's favorite—blustery, sentimental, nuts. Houn'dog, the chauvinist, who is always bursting into tears at the thought of how noble dogs are. Miss Mam'selle Hepzibah, the beautiful skunk with a feisty French independence that makes her more than a match for her many suitors, a feminist thirty years before her time. The three bats, Besmirched, Bothered, and Bewildered. And of course Pogo himself—the wistfully innocent possum with his bedrock common sense that nothing can shake.

Here's a strip that's as typical as any. Albert pushes into shore on a johnboat (in a lovely detail, Kelly always had different names on the boats, honoring his various pals), and is met by Howland Owl, who excitedly explains that they've discovered a baby worm who can write poetry. "Listen, Albert, at the poem that the li'l worm critter wrote out of his own special brain."

The worm recites: "Oh Prettily Preen That Primly Prose That Blooms Amidst The Sunday Snows And Glooms The Glibly Gleaming Glows While Subtly Supping Sweet Suppose."

"By Jing!" Albert responds. "I could write a *better* poem than *that* with *both heads* tied behind of my back!"

"Ohoo!" the worm replies, drawing himself up to his full height. "You missed its fruity import."

"Phoo y'own self . . . It don' mean nothin' an' I don' understan' it."

Howland Owl shrugs. "How can yo' match wits with a worm that got 45 degrees from Paducah U., Glasgow and the Santa Fe R.R.?"

Albert smugly folds his arms. "Bein' a human bean type of alligator, *I* is got 98.6 degrees from FAREN HEIT!"

Kelly's work passes the test of all great satire: It can be appreciated on one level by eight-year-olds, and on another level by savvy adults. For Kelly was one of the great political satirists of the twentieth century; he was among the first in America to take on Joe McCarthy, memorably skewering him as one Simple J. Malarkey, a polecat with a mean five o'clock shadow and a penchant for lynching.

Every four years a reluctant Pogo would be drafted into running for president, resulting in some of the strip's funniest moments. One year he ends up running against a baby bug whose only words are "Jes fine!" The reporters quickly become enamored with him; to every question he's asked about the economy or foreign relations or the future, he answers "Jes fine!," which turns out to be exactly the message the country wants to hear—and a shrewd prediction of the intellectual level to which our campaigns were soon to descend.

Kelly holds up remarkably well. When the news of the world is simply too much to bear, I stagger to my bookshelf and take *Pogo* out, and, like the Bible, you can hardly open it without coming upon some gem of wisdom that helps calm you down. Kelly would write forewords to all the *Pogo* books, and what comes through is an appealing combination of a hard-bitten, hard-drinking, wisecracking old newspaperman of the *Front Page* school, and a wistful, sweet-natured innocent on the order of Pogo himself. Just recently, and for the first time, I heard his voice on an old vinyl record singing "Songs of the Pogo," and his voice is just what you would expect—a bit gruff like Shel Silverstein's, but, withal, oddly gentle and even sweet.

He made *Bartlett's*, of course, for Pogo's most famous pronouncement, the strip in which, seeing all the garbage and pollution leaching its way into the swamp, he sadly proclaims, "We have met the enemy and he is us." But I think if Walt Kelly is looking down now from a watchtower set high above the absurdities of our time, he would prefer any tribute to end with one of his poems, one of the punning Christmas carols—say, for instance, the immortal "Deck Us All With Boston Charlie"—or perhaps with one of his sweeter, more wistful songs, like "A Corner of the Circle" from 1959:

Around in the hoop with the loop of my love
Lies longing my heart sinking low, thinking of
Wonders and magic and worries of woe
With windows all waddled in yesterday's snow
The sun in its tower tolls out the noon
While here in the sphere of the moth-eaten moon
All huddled befuddled with night in the eyes
The Whoop of my heart in its wildness lies.

JEAN SHEPHERD

One of the turning points in young Wetherell's childhood came when he began listening to the radio—not in daylight on his transistor, not on the car radio during family drives, but at night alone in his room with the lights turned off. Darkness wrapped the sound in coziness and wildness at the same time—the sort of mix that gives lovemaking in the dark its allure, though he was a long way from knowing that then. Radio waves travel farther at night, so he would often pull in stations from Toronto or West Virginia, and if the waves traveled farther, couldn't they also travel deeper, boring into his imagination in a way that they simply couldn't manage in the bright light of day?

He would stretch out on his bed under a thick army blanket, the only light being the soft yellow of the radio dial up there on his dresser. His parents would be in bed by this time; there were no sounds in the house except the reassuring white noise of the furnace down in the basement. Outside, via a troubling, red-colored noise, came the sound of sirens, fire horns, and screeching brakes—a surprising amount of these, in a town so tranquil—and he often thought that what he was actually hearing, in that magically amplifying silence, was the frantic buzz of Manhattan twenty miles to the west, the city that never slept.

Pressed between coziness and wildness, his fourteen-year-old soul too restless to allow him to sleep, he listened to the radio with more concentration and absorption than he has ever managed since. Of all the high-tech inventions the twentieth century served up, it was radio, one of the earliest, that would become his favorite. He never liked talking on the phone; computers came along when he was too old to get excited about them; and TV, after its brief golden age, he absolutely detested. It was the future writer in him that fell for radio, with its emphasis on words, the magic way they were transmitted heart to heart, so, like a good novel, it gave you the feeling that it was meant for you and you alone.

Radio, nighttime radio, radio in the dark, would introduce him to assorted wonders he would remain in love with all his life. At his most restless moments, he would turn the dial to find the farthest-away, faintest-sounding station he could possibly feather into. This was AM radio, and in those days the most distant stations were often Canadian ones, playing classical music, very probably the CBC. He had always had generous, benevolent feelings toward Canada (he was a hockey fan, the old six-team NHL; he daydreamed of fishing in Labrador someday; he liked to read books about Arctic exploration), and so he listened to Canadian stations just to feel he wasn't a shy fourteen-year-old kid leading a dull life in The World Capital of Bland, but someone cut out for a serious, strenuous life—listened to them like a prospector temporarily adrift in the city might have listened for a coyote's wild howl.

But it wasn't about howls; he learned that very quickly. It was music, lulling, soft, a whisper of something beautiful scratched across the night. And so he listened, and began learning the names of composers, began recognizing certain tunes, and felt, though it wouldn't fully blossom for another few years, the beginning of a lifelong passion. Listening to those string quartets issuing from what seemed the faraway, tantalizing reaches of the North, he always pictured a cold, well-lit hall in a little Hudson's Bay outpost on the edge of nowhere, the window shining blue in the Borealis, the four musicians huddled in overcoats onstage, faces and instruments reflected in the maple sheen of the floor, bowing away with total commitment on their violins, their viola, their cello. No music before or ever since pierced him so utterly. He can hear them now, those virtuosos of his imagination who produced a sound that was very real. Years later, when he went to his first chamber music recital at Carnegie Hall, he was disappointed somehow with the music, even though it was Isaac Stern and Itzhak Perlman playing—disappointed, he realized, because the sound didn't come coated in static, didn't fade in and out.

His radio sense was very geographic—it wasn't so much the waves reaching him from far distances, but him reaching out with his yearning toward far distances. The farther away the station was, the better he liked what it was playing, and it was only gradually that he realized there was an equal kind of wildness and adventure that lay very close to him, wafting east through the night over the wet, absorbent blanket of those sleeping suburbs. New York stations he was certainly aware of—the Yankees on WCBS with Red Barber; Cousin Brucie or Murray the K on WABC—but the station he one night tuned into was right there in plain sight in the center of the dial, in regions he had never bothered with before: WOR, one of radio's original super stations, with 25,000 watts of power that bullied lesser stations off the air right up and down the Eastern seaboard.

Those were the days when AM radio still programmed mostly music, and one of the reasons he never bothered with WOR was that they had people on who *talked*. Most of the voices were syrupy and/or officious, and he twisted the dial right past them, but on this night the tuning bar stopped on a very different kind of voice. It seemed very close to him in the darkened room—a hoarse voice, wild even, but with an extraordinarily confidential and intimate quality to it. There must have been at least 150,000 fourteen-year-old boys in the greater metropolitan area listening to it just then, and each one of them thought the voice was speaking to him and him alone. The voice, he discovered after only five minutes of listening, was capable of doing extraordinary things, from whispering to yelping to laughing hysterically, often within the space of a single sentence. Its timbre was Midwestern flat, and yet there was some New York wiseguy mixed in, too; this was a voice that came at you from all sorts of directions and depths.

The voice, the man, was talking about how when he was fourteen, he and some friends named Flick and Brunner got up the nerve to sneak into a burlesque house in Chicago, and how he went home afterwards feeling guilty, and writhed in bed all night with a burning sensation in his groin, fearing he had caught something, until he discovered it was only his scratchy new Sears, Roebuck & Co. underwear.

It wasn't until he tuned in the following night that he caught the man's name: Jean Shepherd. He rambled on for forty-five minutes nonstop, saying sarcastic things about the commercials but playing them anyway, then launching into a monologue on something he had read in the paper that day, which led in turn to a story about growing up in Hammond, Indiana, near the steer mills, which segued into a story about his time as a private in the U.S. Signal Corps.

In between breaths, as a kind of filler, he sang Benny Goodman's old hit, "Bei Mir Bist Du Schoen," but with his own version of the lyrics: "The bear missed the train! The bear missed the train! The bear missed the train—and now he's walking!" The stories were absurd, madcap, insightful, tender, crazy . . . his humor was as black as Mort Sahl's or Lenny Bruce's, as exaggerated as Mark Twain's, as gentle as Will Rogers's—a sweetly black humor. For the next five years, from 9:00 PM, when the news, weather, and sports were finished, to 10:00 PM when Shep signed off with his little "Ta-da!," the boy listened to him religiously.

A typical show starts with a bugle call, the kind you hear before a horse race, then his theme comes on, the galloping "Bahn Frei Overture," composed by the one Strauss brother no one's ever heard of. Shepherd's voice emerges: "Okay, gang, are you ready to play the radio game? Are you ready to shuffle off the mortal coil of mediocrity? I am if you are, kiddo." He blows his kazoo . . . *Braap!* . . . or twangs his Jew's harp . . . *Brroing!* . . . "Yes, you meatheads out there in the darkness, you surfers on the Sargasso Sea of existence, take heart, because WOR, in its never-ending crusade of public service, is once again proud to bring you (Beethoven swells in the background) 'The Jean Shepherd Show!'"

Some very obvious, very deliberate fumbling of papers, then Shep reads an item from that day's *Times*: 12 million hams will be sold this year for Easter. His old man, he explains, always loved a good ham, but, being perpetually broke during the Depression, could only afford to buy the family one every year, and that for Easter.

Fine—he floats that out in the air, then suddenly starts singing along with an old honky-tonk record. "I'm the sheik . . . I said the sheik! . . . of Araby! Your love belongs to me . . ."

Midway through the chorus, Shepherd hears police sirens twenty-two stories below in Times Square, and he turns the gain up and throws open the window. "Go get 'em, boys!"

Commercials. Shepherd tells his control man to "push the money button" and a jingle for beer comes on, with Shepherd whistling in tune behind it, and asking rhetorically, at its conclusion, "Isn't it wonderful to be able to measure your happiness in empty flip-top cans?"

Sometimes Shepherd spends all forty-five minutes hopping from subject to subject, but on his best, most memorable nights, his stream-of-consciousness style steers toward a story, albeit one with tangents and stories within stories and random asides. He's talking about dogs now, this crazy mutt named Butcher Boy who his father hated, but his mother would never let him get rid of . . . and then, after another commercial, he's talking about his father again, and how he dreamed all year of buying the Easter ham, saved a bit aside from every paycheck, bought it at just the right butcher's, making the whole event a cere-mony, right down to the careful cooking and carving. You can all but smell and taste that ham, Shepherd has made it so real. It's cooling on the kitchen counter when the family, hearing a plane outside, goes out to watch, that being the era when families still got excited about planes . . .

The young Wetherell and 140,000 boys just like him really get caught up in this, and yet realize, even if they don't have clocks, that it's almost 10:00 now and the story has to end fast. And then, just before Shepherd *does* end it, we all suddenly remember the dog, Butcher Boy, the one he mentioned just in passing so many minutes before— and that's it! The family comes back into the kitchen, his father starts sharpening the carving knife, all but salivating at the prospect of cutting into his prize ham, when they see *it's not there!*—that Butcher Boy is running with it in his jaws, straight out the door!

The tragedy of the stolen ham hangs in the darkness, and then "Keep your knees loose!" Shepherd shouts. The "Bahn Frei Overture" swells back, so time is up now. "By the way, you klutzes that are about to write in saying 'Lay off the philosophy,' you can stop worrying. Tomorrow is an all-kazoo program, friends, and I'm not going to say a word."

That most of Shepherd's fans were teenage boys points to where so much of his appeal rested. Many of these were boys like myself, rest-less as all youth is restless, but with a particularly bad case, caused by their living in the suburbs where, quite literally, nothing ever happened. Shepherd's stories ennobled us; by talking about growing up in Hammond, the bullies, the girls, the misadventures, he was telling us that even our minor adventures were somehow significant, somehow glorious. It was reassuring to know, listening to Shepherd, that one day the little excitements we found in life would become, in retrospect, swollen with meaning, so we would end up having pasts after all, that our lives would be full of similar little comedies and tragedies. Listening to Shepherd, we thought we were night people, hipsters, but what he was really playing on was a sort of anticipatory nostalgia that young teenagers are suckers for. There must be many thousands of men my age who, thanks to Shepherd, now look back on their childhoods in a particularly Shepherdian light.

Was he the funniest man ever on radio? His only competitors were Bob Elliott and Ray Goulding, who were slightly past their prime when I listened to them, since their main topic of satire—radio as it was in the 1940s and '50s—was fast becoming a thing of the past. That said, I would rather play Bob and Ray tapes now than Shepherd's; their humor is drier and yet much more imaginative and absurd, and depends less on the special circumstances of the moment than does Shepherd's. Tippy the Wonder Dog. Garish Summit. Mr. I-Know-Where-They-Are. Wally Ballou, ace reporter. Jack Headstrong, All-American American boy. Bob and Ray's talent for characterization made them the radio equivalent of Charles Dickens.

Patrick McGoohan

The very last shot TV had at young Wetherell before he lost interest in it altogether was with a show imported from Britain: *Secret Agent*, starring Patrick McGoohan. Fronted by absolutely the best theme song any TV show ever had (sung by Johnny Rivers—blue-eyed soul!), the series was about a spy who was a lot more intelligent and graceful than anyone else on view just then, a James Bond without the ego and the gimmicks, with literate scripts that hearkened back to Graham Greene and looked ahead to John le Carré. In one of the early shows, McGoohan, in order to infiltrate a nest of bad guys, has to seduce a mysterious, gamine French *chanteuse* in dark sunglasses, and since the boy was already a big fan of mysterious, gamine French *chanteuses* in dark sunglasses, this made an immediate impression on him. *Secret Agent* quickly became his favorite show.

McGoohan was a remarkable actor, capable of a lot more than playing spies (he once costarred in a London stage production of *Moby-Dick* with none other than Orson Welles), but he never condescended to the role, and he played it with a thinking man's intelligence and wit. He wasn't drop-dead handsome, at least not in the Sean Connery mode; if anything, he was a sort of average-looking bloke, and the charisma he exuded came entirely from the force of his character.

After the series had ended its run, he produced, directed, and starred in *The Prisoner*, the cult favorite that was probably the strangest, most experimental series ever aired to that point. He begins as a character very similar to what he played in *Secret Agent*, but then, after some unexplained infraction, he's kidnapped and taken to a very odd, very rococo "village," where he can reside in safety as long as he never tries to escape. He tries to escape, of course—in each episode, he tries different methods, but is always captured by a giant bubble (!) and taken back.

McGoohan plays this with a sustained fury that remains mostly inward, with the expression you would see on a man who, whatever his surface mood, never ceases fighting. There is a kind of manly intellectualism in those dark, open eyes, a vague cynicism that is smart enough to be skeptical about its own cynicism, and this is exactly the quality that McGoohan brought to this role. He wins his freedom eventually by sheer endurance and this steady, moral refusal to give in.

For the young teenager, this was heady stuff. There is a kind of admiration that is never spoken of much, because of fears of being misunderstood. Boys can get a crush on older men in a way that has nothing to do with sex (well, at least not until the third or fourth psychological level beneath the surface). It's platonic, but very real. You want to have the older boy or man notice you, approve of you, and this eventually leads to emulation—you want to be like him, look like him, move like him, talk like him, act like him—the whole admiring, hero-worshipping nine yards. Almost every boy in his young teens experiences something like this, and, for this particular boy, Patrick McGoohan was the one he fell for hardest, to the point where even today when he's faced with a situation requiring grace under pressure, he remembers McGoohan in *Secret Agent* or *The Prisoner* . . . and it's via these devices, this nostalgic playacting, that a grown man copes.

Benedict Arnold

Young Wetherell's boyish admiration for soldiers, particularly those of lieutenant-general rank or higher, lingered for a surprisingly long time. It was given a boost by the centennial of the Civil War, which was being celebrated in the usual American way: an avalanche of articles and TV programs leading up to it, numerous ceremonies during 1961, the centennial year itself, and then, over the course of the next four years, more muted, localized commemorations as this battle and then that one was remembered. It should be noted that there was noticeably less interest on the part of a public who, with Vietnam beginning to dominate the headlines, quickly wearied of a hundred-year-old war. What the boy would remember were the newspaper articles as the last surviving veterans from the war died off. In 1957, the very last survivor died—a centenarian who had been a fourteen-year-old drummer boy during the war, or the same age as the boy reading about him with such empathy and interest.

His fascination with the Civil War was short-lived, but very intense. His parents, wanting to encourage his love of history, took the family down to Pennsylvania for a tour of the Gettysburg battlefield, even hiring a guide to drive them around. The boy, who wasn't usually like that, began showing off how much he already knew about the battle, adding informative little tangents to the guide's main points. The guide, a kindly soul who wore a hat like a state trooper's, kept marveling at this, which made the boy burst with pride.

The danger in becoming a Civil War buff, of course, is that you begin mourning for the Lost Cause and end up rooting for the South to win. The boy avoided this danger, but barely. Lee, Jackson, Longstreet, Early, Mosby—they were indeed a colorful, compelling crew. He read about them all he could, took *Lee's Lieutenants* out from the library, all but memorized *Death of a Nation* by Clifford Dowdey—rooted, more than he had ever rooted for his favorite sports teams, for Pickett's men to reach that little grove of trees and thereby penetrate the Union center, all but sobbed as Massa Lee took all the blame on his shoulders as the Army of Northern Virginia retreated back over the Potomac once again.

Yes, the lost, eternally bittersweet cause . . . but then, quite suddenly, he turned against it and came to his senses. Rooting for the South went against all his finer instincts, which, nurtured by a Puritan residue deep in his soul, were being stoked by the civil rights movement into something fierce and unforgiving. He now saw Lee as nothing but a slave monger too caught up in his Romantic notions of pride and duty to see which way the historical wind was blowing, becoming the tool of the hotheaded South Carolina planters who had started the war for their own personal gain. A Radical Republican—that's what the boy eventually turned into when it came to the Civil War.

Something deep and mysterious in him still needed to admire a general, and it was entirely characteristic of who he was at the time that he ended up with Benedict Arnold. Who better fit the role of anti-hero than Arnold, who was definitely *not* the kind of person they wrote about in Childhoods of Famous Americans. The boy, in his restless quest to read every book on the Hempstead Public Library shelves, had found his way to the historical novels of Kenneth Roberts, *Arundel* and *Rabble in Arms*, which were compelling re-creations of the campaigns fought in the North during 1775 and 1776, told through the eyes of a young man named Steven Nason, who in the books wasn't that much older than the boy himself.

To Nason, marching through the Maine woods to attack Quebec, or serving on board one of the American ships Arnold commanded at Valcour Island, Arnold was a hero of the first rank, incredibly brave, resolute, with a fury in battle that awed everyone who witnessed it, Americans and Britons alike. When Arnold turned traitor, Nason cut him an enormous amount of slack, justifying his actions with all the abuse and neglect he suffered at the hands of Congress and jealous superiors like Horatio Gates—justifications that the young teenage Wetherell had no trouble swallowing. Kenneth Roberts wrote:

Arnold was a brave and gallant gentleman, who, if it had not been for the terrible thing that later happened, would be acknowledged by all soldiers to be a very great man, second only to General Washington in daring and brilliance in military matters; for he had all of the qualities of a very great soldier—observation, right judgement, quickness, leadership,

determination, energy and courage—and all of this, it seemed
to me, in the highest degree . . . In none of my readings have
I ever learned of a man so villainously persecuted and disappointed and unrewarded as this brave and gallant gentleman,
or of a man so persistently deprived of his just rewards.

In retrospect, this is a bit worrying—that a boy could have worshipped
a knave like Benedict Arnold. And while it's tempting to laugh off the
boy's Arnold craze, or his enthusiasm for the Confederates, he would
sometimes wonder in later years if this wasn't a dangerous and tricky
point in his life where he could have become a lifelong Conservative,
someone who sneered at the masses and found his champions in the
ranks of the ruthlessly right wing. A true believer he was never cut out
to be, in any creed or dogma, but there was another route that may have
led him into the Conservative camp; he was the kind of young person
who was beginning to see through many pretensions, pretensions of
all sorts, so it's entirely possible he could have grown into the kind of
Conservative, quite common in his experience, who adopts their political stance simply because they see through liberal hypocrisies better
than they do Conservative ones. This is the kind of Conservative who
would find admirable things to say about Benedict Arnold or Bedford
Forrest or Joseph McCarthy, just to get a liberal's easily gotten goat.

It was only gradually, reading further, that the boy came to understand the depth of Arnold's treachery; indeed, he may have been the last
American to ever feel personally betrayed by Benedict Arnold—but the
hurt caused by this, politically speaking, did him a world of good.

My infatuation with Arnold was ludicrously misplaced—and yet, to
give my younger self credit, I at least focused in on one of the most
interesting figures from American history. No biographer has ever fully
explored the inner geography of Benedict Arnold's heart. The springs
from whence flowed his mad, desperate courage lie so close to the
sources of his cynical, calculated treachery that the channels quickly
merge, making it impossible to follow the bravery without being over-
whelmed by the darkness—which makes him, to our lasting fascination
and bewilderment, among the hardest human beings to understand in
American history.

I'll still admit to a sneaking admiration for him. A few years back, I coaxed my wife Celeste into taking an "Arnold drive" to visit some relatively nearby landmarks associated with his career. We picked up Arnold's trail near Skowhegan, Maine, the gritty mill town near the falls of the Kennebec River that was the Quebec expedition's first major obstacle. The route they followed leads toward Stratton/Eustis on the notorious "Height of Land," the mountain hump that tilts the watersheds toward Canada. The Appalachian Trail crosses the highway near Mount Bigelow (named for one of Arnold's officers), and we took a hike there just to get an appreciation of what marching through this forest, with no trails, must have been like. Even as late as the 1930s, local woodsmen could tell which way Arnold's army had gone by the line of hardwoods that had sprung up after Arnold's axmen had hewn down the original spruce.

This is lonely country still, and surely the only corner of the world where Arnold is still remembered as a hero. The gas station in Stratton is called "The Arnold Trail Service Station"; there's "Arnold Pond" near where Maine becomes Canada; and then, once you cross the border, the "Rivière Arnold" which runs underneath Highway 161. My wife and I were delighted to find not one motel, but *two* named after him in Quebec: the simple Motel Arnold in Saint-Augustin-de-Woburn, and the upscale Auberge Motel Benedict Arnold in Ville de Saint-Georges, in Beauce—Beauce, in 1775, being the first inhabited town on the Chaudière River, and the place where Arnold, racing ahead of his men, bought the cattle from the Quebecois farmers that saved his men from starvation.

We spent the night in Quebec, where Arnold was wounded beneath the walls of the inner city, and then drove down Lake Champlain to see where he had fought his fleet through eight hours' worth of brutal pounding at Valcour Island. We ended up at the battlefield at Saratoga—for me, one of the most evocative of American places. At one corner of a gentle meadow here, shaded by trees and not at first obvious, is one of the strangest battlefield monuments ever erected: a beautifully sculpted leg, elegantly booted, standing by itself on what appears to be a cannon, beneath which a short, nameless inscription explains—and doesn't explain—what it commemorates:

IN MEMORY OF THE MOST BRILLIANT SOLDIER OF THE CONTINENTAL
ARMY WHO WAS DESPERATELY WOUNDED ON THIS SPOT, WINNING FOR
HIS COUNTRYMEN THE DECISIVE BATTLE OF THE AMERICAN REVOLU-
TION AND FOR HIMSELF THE RANK OF MAJOR GENERAL.

As the fighting broke out here on October 7, Arnold had been relieved
of his command by Horatio Gates, forced to stand idle as a spectator
while his best troops came up against stiff British resistance and the
battle's outcome seemed suddenly in doubt.

This seems the key moment in Arnold's life, and it's important to
try to understand what was in his heart as he rode back and forth on
his charger, forbidden to take part in the battle, and yet compelled by
a fury he was powerless to stop. The fury came from so many sources,
so much hurt and so much courage, that it's almost impossible to
comprehend—but surely part of it was his overwhelming sense that
this landscape, this great northern corridor, was *his*. Hadn't he won
it for himself on the excruciating march through the wilderness, or on
the dark snowy streets of Quebec, or along the Richelieu on the bitter
retreat, or at the glory of Valcour Island? This was *his* land, to defend
to the last drop of his being—his to win for his country, his, ultimately,
to one day sell for good British gold.

Arnold finds it impossible to resist his own courage. He gathers up
some men, leads the vital charge that wins the redoubt for the Americans
and seals the victory—and, just as he crashes into the redoubt, is shot in
the same leg that was wounded in Quebec.

Historians for years have always made the point that it would have
been better for Arnold's reputation had he been killed at the peak of his
glory in Saratoga—and yet perhaps they miss the point. In a very real
sense, he *was* killed at Saratoga, the good Arnold, the one that for two
brilliant years courageously overrode all his demons . . . and almost
certainly Arnold sensed this himself.

Henry Dearborn rushes up to him, asks where he's been shot. "In
the leg," Arnold tells him—and then, he utters what is surely one of the
saddest lines in American history: "I wish it had been my heart."

Lives of the Saints

HENRY DAVID THOREAU

You can be a dilettante in admiration like you can be a dilettante in all of the passions that make life bearable. Almost everyone grows up worshipping a catalog of favorites, some of whom, over the long haul, turn out to be keepers, but in a golden-oldies kind of way that involves mainly nostalgia. This is harmless, natural—but not for the serious-minded, those who in youth strove to emerge from the indignities of common life and achieve great things. For them, to end up being merely a "fan" can be tormenting.

The boy, inspired by Gandhi in his youth, wanted to use his idealism to help end war. Years later, having turned to more mundane pursuits, he feels a flush of disappointment and shame when he hears the name "Gandhi," knowing that his admiration, so intense when he was sixteen, turned after all to nothing.

A girl inspired by Billie Holliday, wanting more than anything to make music her life, finds that it's too hard, too demanding, requiring a single-minded dedication her friends and parents absolutely refuse to understand—and so, following the path of least resistance, she becomes just another housewife, just another doctor, just another this or that. She'll still have her Billie Holliday records, will even play them occasionally, but less and less so as she nears fifty, since their vinyl has become coated over the years with the thick, bitter dust of what-might-have-been.

Admiration's higher purpose should be to inspire you, guide you, stimulate you, point and prod you toward certain directions, support your efforts to achieve great things. Or at least that's what admiration should be doing for ardent young people. It's at fourteen or fifteen that this kind of ambition often starts, sometimes as faint stirrings of free-floating admiration that may not attach itself to any particular hero or mentor . . . and at other times more explicitly, more explosively, finding someone we admire so much that they end up converting us to their side, in the broadest possible meaning of "conversion." You can be a fan and leave it at that, or you can be a follower—and how closely to follow, with what degree of adherence, can take an entire lifetime to puzzle out.

How far should you let admiration take you? Should it color you, shape you, mold you, spit you back out changed to your very core—or should it be a tamer, drier thing, something you keep safe in the closet of memory but don't often bring to light? It's not just a hypothetical question, not when you're fourteen and all but bursting with unrequited moral fervor. The boy, this young Wetherell, having gone through the puppy-love stage of admiration, was now about to fall in love for real.

It's a puzzle where and when he first encountered the name "Thoreau." It definitely was *not* in school. Hawthorne and Melville were included in the syllabus, and Walt Whitman was probably mentioned, too, since he was born farther out on Long Island (near the "Walt Whitman Shopping Mall"), but Emerson wasn't included, let alone Thoreau. Were they looked upon as far too radical or diffi-cult? Thoreau's reputation had experienced some ups and downs since his death—the affluent, unquestioning postwar years were one of his relative down spots—so perhaps the boy's English teachers were hardly even aware of him.

For a young person to find a dead author, posterity has to do its job, and, with Thoreau, this had been far from automatic. His books were ignored when he was living, and if Emerson and other literary big shots admired him, it was with more than a little condescension. Nature lovers took him up after his death, but badly emasculated him, portraying him as a shy "bachelor of nature," who, in the opinion of *The New York Times* circa 1865, "sought a cold and selfish isolation from human cares and interests."

Luckily, a Michigan osteopath named Dr. Samuel Jones fell in love with his work, and devoted an immense amount of effort to ensuring that Thoreau's writings were not forgotten. Between 1889 (thirty-five years after Thoreau's death) and 1907, Jones exchanged hundreds of letters with other Thoreau admirers, including Alfred Hosmer back in Massachusetts, and nature writer H. S. Salt in England, keeping everyone abreast of new developments in Thoreau's growing reputation, dissing Emerson, publishing appreciative essays in one obscure journal after another, journeying to Concord to meet with the yet-living among Thoreau's contemporaries, including, on one memorable visit, Sam Staples, the genial jailer who had once locked Thoreau up.

Dr. Jones himself is all but forgotten, but in the history of admiration he deserves an honored spot. Here's a very typical quote from a letter Jones wrote in 1890 to one of Thoreau's still living friends:

> Thoreau is generally regarded as a sour, crabbed cynic. Now I never saw any photograph of Thoreau, and no steel engraving can give the eyes as a photograph does, yet I feel in my heart that, if one were absolutely an earnest and sincere man, he would find in Thoreau an infinite depth of tenderness. Not the demonstrative kind, but that which you *see* in the eyes and feel warming your own heart. Am I right? I do not want to burden your age with writing a letter, but a reply from you, if only a word, will do my heart good, and I ask it from pure love for Thoreau.

So, thanks to disciples like Jones, posterity had done its job, keeping Thoreau alive into the early 1960s, where it was at least theoretically possible for a young person to find him—but, again, who exactly made the match for young Wetherell?

Most likely it was a reference in the work of one of the amateur naturalists, who, writing for New York newspapers during the week, spent weekends at their cabins in Connecticut, communing with nature—and then writing about it in lightly lyrical essays that eventually found their way back to the boy, in their newspapers or magazines. Brooks Atkinson, the famous Broadway critic; John Kiernan, the sportswriter; Hal Borland, who wrote the nature editorials in the *Times*—even E. B. White, who still kept one foot in the city even as he wrote about rural Maine. They were the local nature popularizers of his day; they worshipped Thoreau, so it was almost certainly in their writings that the fourteen-year-old Wetherell first encountered his name.

Encountered the name—and took in the single most important fact about him: that he had lived alone in a cabin by a pond. To the boy, already world-weary at fourteen, in love with fishing, a great admirer of ducks and geese, this seemed like absolutely the best idea he had ever heard of, and he became enchanted with the notion of *Walden* before reading a single line.

He got his parents to drive him to the local department store, A & S's, where in the book section he found not quite exactly what he was looking for. *The Variorum Walden* was the title on the paperback; he had no idea what "variorum" meant, but it had a nice distinguished ring to it, and the "Walden" attached to it cinched the purchase. On the car ride home, he scanned the introduction by Walter Harding (he was a sucker for anything written by a Walter), and learned that "variorum" meant a facsimile of the first edition, with copious explanatory notes. And this turned out to be a good thing, since whenever the prose became a little difficult for him, he could relax with the footnotes—and then a few weeks later, on a trip to a real bookstore, he found the Modern Library $4.95 edition of *Walden and other Writings*, with an introduction by Brooks Atkinson—and this is the book—the cover of which (a strong man framed between trees, hand on a walking staff, staring pensively toward a distant pond), the typeface, the little rips and tears, the well-thumbed pages, the soda and tea stains, the memorized paragraphs—that engraved itself on his life.

He read it that first time, as young people will, strictly as a story. A man goes to live by a small New England pond, builds a cabin there, plants beans, has some visitors, thinks about eating a woodchuck raw, leaves the pond. As far as the plot goes, it's very simple, and the boy may even have been a little bit disappointed. He had invested a great deal of patience in the actual reading—Thoreau's prose is remarkably modern, but demanding enough to force the boy to stretch—and he would have liked a bit more in the way of detail on things like what kind of bait he used in pickerel fishing, or if he ever got scared at night when there were thunderstorms.

But even on that first reading, working on him without his being fully aware of it, Thoreau's magic came across. Any sensitive young reader, finding their way to Thoreau, responds to this—an inarticulate quality, an essential honesty, a clarity, a passion, that seems to float just below the words themselves, strong and buoyant enough to make you fall in love with Thoreau before you fully understand what the words mean. "Purity" is a loaded word, an invitation to sarcasm, but it's there in Thoreau, all right—the genuine article—and perhaps it's only a young person who can match it, like for like.

Having read *Walden* that first time, the young man immediately read it again. He didn't need anyone to underline the best parts—he found on his own the passages which have stirred so many:

> I went to the woods because I wished to live deliberately, to front only the essential facts of life, and see if I could not learn what it had to teach, and not, when I came to die, discover that I had not lived . . . Time is the stream I go a-fishing in. I drink at it, but while I drink I see the sandy bottom and detect how shallow it is. Its thin current slides away, but eternity remains . . . If you stand right fronting and face to face with a fact, you will see the sun glimmer on both its surfaces, and feel its sweet edge dividing you through the heart and marrow. Be it life or death, we crave only reality.

Thoreau's "message," heady enough when read in the bland, shriveled heart of suburbia, took on doubled power when his parents bought a small summer house in the woods near a Connecticut lake. He had his *Walden* with him when they first drove north to see it, and yes, there was his Walden down a wooded hill right outside what was going to be his bedroom. Water, the tricks of beauty it plays, is the key element in Thoreau's writings, and, thanks to having a lake nearby, it would become the favorite medium of this impressionable young man—still water, moving water, water that was whitecapped, sun-flecked and living. Even his love of fishing sprang from this; that trout and bass live in *water*, not meadows or woods, was always the point for him. "Earth's eyes," Thoreau famously said of ponds, and Wetherell, in the next fifty years, was going to devote an ungodly amount of hours staring into those eyes as deeply as he could.

There is no exaggerating the influence Thoreau had on him, coming along at just the right time, at fourteen, when stirrings, inclinations, instincts fly off in so many different directions that only the strongest magnet can focus them into a beam. Thanks to Thoreau, the young man thought favorably of nonconformity, wanted to do whatever it took to live his own life and not the one expected of him. Thanks to Thoreau, he wanted no part of the corporate world, no desk job, no business. Thanks to Thoreau, he learned to watch for the beauty that resides in small, easily overlooked moments—how snow coats the branches of a maple after a storm, for instance, making explicit the intricate pattern, swelling the tapering tips, revealing a latent beauty that drabness usually hides.

Thanks to Thoreau, all his Romantic yearnings became fixed on the country, not the city; he didn't long, like so many provincials before him, to move to New York or London, but as deep into the boonies as he could manage. Thanks to Thoreau, he would rent many cold, drafty cabins to do his writing in. Thanks to Thoreau, he learned that good prose has a cadence and rhythm that isn't just there for show, but to double the impact of words, underlining them, giving them depth and fullness like snow on maple branches. He learned that lyric prose should be ballasted by preciseness to keep it from blowing off those branches too easily, too soon. Thanks to Thoreau, he wanted to become a writer who celebrated life, not just moaned.

Is that admiration enough? Reading back these last few paragraphs, remembering Thoreau's impact, it sounds far too sober. To Thoreau, the young man owed *everything*—and even that seems like a timid understatement.

Thoreau, who died in his forties, has always been considered a young person's writer, both in his eloquent lyricism and in his call for revolution in how a person holds himself to the world. Someone like me, reading him again in late middle age, is apt to feel too comfortable and settled, too smug, to be able to withstand Thoreau's sting. In the last ten years, Thoreau had become someone I remembered loving, but whose lessons weren't particularly relevant to the present-day conditions of my life.

I'm a father, a husband; the chief concern of my forties and fifties has been my family. In all the two-million-plus words of Thoreau's remarkable journal, you will find hardly any mention of children (though in person he was the most popular leader of berry-picking expeditions in Concord), and he hardly writes about women at all, except favorites like the elderly and wise Miss Mary Emerson. Dying young, middle-age responsibilities—and middle-age staleness and ennui—are things he never had to deal with.

And yet, when I finally got back to him, something remarkable happens: My heart turns out to be young enough to leap toward Thoreau's words and embrace them all over again; they can still send shivers down my spine, elicit a visceral response no other author can duplicate. Delight, inspiration, amusement (it's fun rediscovering Thoreau's marvelously dry sense of humor), recognition—all of these are waiting inside his books like flowers I pressed there thirty years ago, and which, released now, spring back to glorious life.

And something harder, more demanding than a flower. "In wildness is the preservation of the world," he famously wrote, and it's easy to forget his own wildness, his rebelliousness, his passionate nonconformity. That's where the biggest surprise comes in rereading Thoreau—how challenging, radical, even dangerous he seems now.

"Civil Disobedience" was not just the name of an essay for Thoreau, his own private declaration of independence, but it was a protest he engaged in at least three times in his life. Sheltering fugitive slaves. Refusing to pay his poll tax. Helping (although Thoreau's biographers barely mention this) Francis Jackson Merriam, one of John Brown's raiders (and thus, a wanted "terrorist"), escape to Canada.

After this, when Brown was hung, Thoreau delivered his angriest speech ever, "In Defense of Captain John Brown." This, even for the relatively liberal Concord citizens, was going too far—it's as if Michael Moore suddenly began producing videos for Osama bin Laden. The timid selectmen refused to ring the town bell to announce the meeting where he read this speech, so Thoreau, nothing daunted, rang it himself. When even the local abolitionist society sent word that such a speech was premature, he replied, in words that ring braver than any bell, "I did not send to you for advice, but to announce that I am to speak."

That's the Thoreau who means the most to me now, the radical, dissenting Thoreau, the one who not only revolted against the cowardly habits of living we all fall into, but against the craven society that heedlessly destroys so much. "No man in America,' he writes, in words meant to describe John Brown, but which could fittingly be applied to himself, "has ever stood up so persistently and effectively for the dignity of human nature, knowing himself for a man, and the equal of any and all governments. In that sense he was the most American of us all."

PETE SEEGER

In the early winter of 1963, at a Long Island Rail Road station called "Country Life Press," a middle-aged, respectable-looking mother and father could have been seen doing a generous and remarkable thing. These war veterans, these Republicans, these decent and happily conventional suburbanites, were taking their son into New York City to attend a Pete Seeger concert—Seeger, the champion of every progressive cause on the map, the union agitator, the Communist sympathizer, the scourge of the House Un-American Activities Committee, the blacklisted enemy. Generous, because they knew how much their son idolized him; remarkable, because they hardly went into the city at all, except for the Radio City Christmas show and an occasional Broadway matinee. Neither of them had ever been to Carnegie Hall before, so perhaps that was part of the draw, but it was their son who was the prime mover, their son whose passion they were encouraging.

His father still knew the subway from his time working in Manhattan immediately after the war, and it was impressive how, once they made it to Penn Station, he found them the correct train uptown. They ate dinner at Schrafft's on 57th Street—the safe family choice of those years. Carnegie Hall had just been saved from demolition by the efforts of the famous violinist Isaac Stern, and, once inside, it reminded them of their Congregational church back home, with the same kind of dignified austerity and cream-colored trim.

It was the people sitting in the seats that they had no reference for. The tidal wave of the '60s—what the '60s looked like, dressed like, acted like, went down in history like—had definitely *not* reached their part of

Long Island in 1964, but it engulfed Carnegie Hall that night, at least with Pete Seeger as the draw. Old leftists and their offspring, the flower children of tomorrow—they took up every seat, dangled their legs over the balcony, exploded into shouts as a very slender man dressed in work clothes, a banjo slung upside down over his shoulder, a twelve-string guitar cradled underneath his arm, walked shyly onstage. He stared absentmindedly into the lights, plucked a banjo string or two, hummed a few bars of nothing in particular, then, thrusting his head out, broke into song.

My god, the boy decided, looking down at him from their seats. *Henry David Thoreau!*

And yes, there was definitely a resemblance—if Thoreau had been reincarnated as a folksinger, he would definitely have turned out to be Pete Seeger (though Seeger's own favorite nineteenth-century soul brother was always Johnny Appleseed). They looked alike—lean, almost gaunt, with nothing superfluous in posture or expression, and tremendous character radiating down the forehead, nose, and chin—and their Puritan-based, dissenting moral fervor twinned them as well.

His first song may very well have been "Down by the Riverside," the old spiritual cum antiwar song and, as was Seeger's way, he got the audience singing right along with him, divvying everyone up into sopranos, altos, and basses, waving his arm from left to right to cue sections in when it came their turn, yelling out exhortations ("I can't hear ya!") to inspire us on. Seeger was a genius at this, and if there were any doubts on this score before that night, then the fact he got the boy's parents singing along, too, even on the union songs, the rabidly antiwar ones, was the ultimate proof.

It was a great concert, an ever-memorable night—the first time young Wethcrell had ever seen any of his heroes actually perform live on a stage. And his parents, world-class good sports, had a great time, too—they even joined in the standing ovation after Seeger finished with his famous "Wimoweh" yodel.

The young man had first learned about Pete Seeger at his friend Mike Scheffler's house. The Schefflers were not just the only family he knew who had lots of books and records in their house, but they were also the first actual Democrats he had ever met in the flesh. Some of their LPs were by The Weavers, Seeger's famous quartet, and the songs he remembered hearing first were from their reunion concert at Carnegie Hall. At the same time, like everyone else then, he was hearing about a group called Peter, Paul and Mary; two of their first hits, "Where Have All the Flowers Gone?" and "The Hammer Song," turned out to have been written by the same man who sang in The Weavers, Pete Seeger. The folk boom's second wave was just starting (the first, fronted by energetic frat boys like The Kingston Trio, was giving way to better stuff), and while Dylan and Baez were names he hadn't quite heard of yet, folk music had become a lot more interesting to him than the rock he had never particularly cared for.

Something that especially intrigued him was that every time he saw the name "Pete Seeger" anywhere, it was always preceded by the article "the" and the adjective "legendary." "The legendary Pete Seeger"—it seemed his official name. Nowadays, "legendary" is attached to everyone and everything, but in those days it still had some meaning, and it made him curious—legendary for what? And he found an ironic path to Seeger, too. On Long Island, in a case that was getting much attention in the papers, a local high school had canceled a Seeger concert under pressure from the American Legion—and so efforts to blacklist him and silence him had the happy effect of helping turn one Long Island teenager into a lifelong Seeger fan.

This was in the early '60s, before that memorable Carnegie Hall visit. Next time his parents went to A & S's, he pocketed his allowance and went along, taking the escalator to the record section on the third floor—and yes, this bastion of American consumerism had Seeger all right; fifty years later, when he took the vinyl records out to play over again, the jackets still had little white A & S price tags affixed to the top.

The first album he bought was one in the long series Seeger did for Folkways, *Great American Songs and Ballads*, his interpretation of everything that could remotely be labeled an American folk song. A photo on the back let him study Seeger's face before plopping down his money. He had a distinctively shaped head, large, with a skeletal prominence above the eyes and temples, counterbalanced by unblemished, baby-smooth skin, to the point that, even at forty, his face suggested both wisdom and youth. A saint's face, not so much self-absorbed as wryly curious. A face better suited to expressing pain than joy, so it was good he had his music to tip the balance the happier way.

As for Seeger's voice, listening that first time when he put the record on his hi-fi, it surprised the young man greatly, being simpler, less honeyed than what he'd expected—what he'd expected being something on the order of Burl Ives. "A true, untrained voice" is how Seeger described it himself, and he was right, especially about the "true" part. Never was a voice better suited to conveying sincerity than Pete Seeger's. It was a high baritone, close enough to a tenor that it had a tenor's very specialized appeal; growing up, it was likely he had been influenced by Bing Crosby or Gene Autry, since he could put a surprisingly sweet croon into his timbre if the song called for it. Compared to Dylan, it was Caruso, and there was none of that overweening narcissism you had in Dylan. It was a passionate voice, too; who would think, looking at that gaunt, Puritan visage, that it could ever sing with such full-throated ardency?

Seeger would always joke about his voice, but its honesty appealed to the boy instantly, its remarkable flexibility and range (no other male singer of those years, with the possible exception of Roy Orbison, could have sung "Wimoweh" like he did). Whatever else it was, it was definitely *his* voice, his character, and the boy fell in love with the sound the way people fell in love with Sinatra's or Tony Bennett's sound. A great deal of nonsense surrounds the phrase "voice of the people," but, if the American people, working people, were somehow given a single characteristic voice to sing with, colored and forged by 300 years of their experience, who else's could that voice be but Pete Seeger's?

The first album played so often its grooves became grooved, Wetherell went back to A & S's and bought a second, then nearly every album Seeger put out—and he put out dozens—over the course of the next six years. Between the ages of thirteen and nineteen, while his contemporaries were moving from Dave Seville and the Chipmunks to Connie Francis to The Beatles to Simon and Garfunkel to The Rolling Stones, Pete Seeger supplied the ever-present soundtrack to his life, and there could have been few times in his house when, with his door closed to spare his parents and sister, he wasn't singing along with another of

Seeger's songs, or trying, via Seeger's "How to Play the 5-string Banjo," to teach himself to play, too.

"Keep your eyes on the prize, hold on! Hold on! Hold on! Keep your eyes on the prize, HOLD ON!" the boy would sing, pumping his fist in the air as if he were standing alone on the Carnegie Hall stage, getting 2,000 people to sing along with him.

Seeger, unlike the singer/songwriters that came after, recorded hundreds of songs written by other composers, from anonymous Appalachian folk songs to the latest Joni Mitchell. This breadth of repertoire meant that, in listening to him, Wetherell learned a lot of things about a lot of subjects that he would never hear about in school— as a source of historical information from the forgotten, "losers" side of history, Seeger simply couldn't be beat. The Wobblies. Grand Coulee Dam. The Spanish Civil War. Pretty Boy Floyd. The Battle of Bennington. Aimee Semple McPherson. Joe Hill. The Scottsboro Boys. Harlan County. Deportees. José Marti. The USS *Reuben James*. These, and a hundred other references, first came to his attention via Seeger's songs, prodded his curiosity, made him want to learn more.

It's the sheer quantity of this music, Seeger's staggering breadth of reference, that hits you hardest looking back on his work. If you take just the albums the boy would end up saving all his life, write down the song titles, stream them impressionistically together, you end up with a "found" prose poem that carries you through broad, exhilarating swaths of the American experience:

> *If you miss me at the back of the bus a hard rain's a'gonna fall who killed Davy Moore little boxes oh freedom what did you learn in school today Guantanamera mail myself to you waist deep in the big muddy seek and you shall find last night I had the strangest dream East Virginia my name is Lisa Kalvelage melodie d'amour sailing down my golden river those three on are on my mind the hammer song we are soldiers in the army Michael row the boat ashore don't want your millions mister bourgeois blues talking union the D-Day dodgers what a friend we have in congress green grows the grass we shall overcome kisses sweeter than wine oh had I a golden thread turn turn turn Jefferson and liberty boll weevil raise a ruckus tonight*

America the beautiful dark as a dungeon talking un-American
blues blood on the saddle Kevin Barry putting on the style oh
Mary don't you weep big rock candy mountain.

Critics were right when they said there was always a subliminal message in Seeger's music, but they were wrong on what that message said. The predominant element in all these songs was hope—hope for humanity, hope that the world would one day be better, if only mankind could find the courage not to give up. This is a message that can work powerfully on a young person, since it matches perfectly with the moral inclinations a young heart fights toward on its own. Seeger, like Thoreau, would turn out to be one of the teenager's most important teachers, making sure his instincts always favored the underdog, the lonely courageous, those who refuse to go along with the status quo. Playing Seeger's music, like reading Thoreau's prose, steered the boy into a life of quiet and stubborn rebellion from the drab suburban fate life had mapped out for him—and just because it was so quiet, so personal, so difficult and lonely, it ended up that the rebellion succeeded, where so many of his contemporaries, after their flashy joint rebellions of the '60s, surrendered into the life of quiet desperation that had been waiting to ensnare them all along.

ROSA PARKS

Seeger and Thoreau, between them, taught the young man to keep his eyes on two kinds of moral courage: Thoreau, to admire the brave, solitary souls who stand up against the establishment in personal acts of rebellion; Seeger, to admire the ones who, feeling the same sense of moral outrage, organize others to fight with them. Thoreau's hero is John Brown, the "terrorist" of his day, who could never enlist more than a few followers; Seeger's hero is Joe Hill, the famous union organizer. Someone in their teens is apt to relate more to Thoreau's solitary kind of moral courage. Standing up to a bully, resisting peer pressure, speaking out with an unpopular opinion in a hostile or indifferent class—these are the kinds of moral challenges sixteen-year-olds are apt to face.

And so, when the civil rights movement reached the critical mass needed to capture a suburban teenager's attention, it was the solitary heroes of the movement that struck him hardest: Rosa Parks refusing to give up her seat on a Montgomery bus in 1955, or James Meredith walking alone to register for classes at Ole Miss in 1962—the solitary ones, or the ones who braved things out with just a handful of supporters: the students marching within their ring of soldiers to enter Little Rock Central High in 1957; Chaney, Goodman, and Schwerner registering voters along the dark backwoods roads of rural Mississippi during the Freedom Summer of 1964.

When it came to demonstrating true moral courage, nothing else in his era even came close to the civil rights movement. Historically speaking, selfishly speaking, it came along at just the right moment in his moral development, so he, a white boy living in an all-white suburb, imprinted on the movement the way an orphan puppy raised by a cat becomes completely feline. Long after the tumult of those years, it became fashionable to pooh-pooh the marches, sit-ins, and demonstrations, saying that the system of racial oppression, after relaxing slightly, snapped shut again in a vicious backlash that isn't over yet. This ignores the huge number of people in this country, white and black, who were forever changed by the heroism and leadership of a relative handful. The antiwar protests, the marches for women's rights, the conservation movement—even obscure and unrecorded acts of tolerance and empathy. The people who engaged in these learned their lessons in courage from people like Rosa Parks.

And what's odd, though her name is iconic today, is that the boy we're talking about here may not have actually known it at the time, in 1955, when her famous act of disobedience took place. What he did know, thanks to the newspaper, was that a polite, pleasant-looking black woman, riding home from a long day's work, had refused to give up her seat in the whites-only section of the bus. This was segregation, moral wrong, in its most easily understood manifestation. The boy rode buses to school every day, and he knew that where you sat in them was a huge issue; a definite pecking order was in place, and it took moral and physical courage to challenge it. And so Rosa Parks, even before he caught and remembered her name, seemed the bravest person he had ever heard of.

One of the interesting results of the new psychological study of admiration mentioned in the introduction is their finding that admiration and compassion come from adjacent, closely matched areas in the brain—and so the teenager's sympathy for the poor woman being ejected from her seat may have leaked over to admiration very quickly. According to the Brain and Creativity Institute, "Compassion for social pain and admiration for virtue, perhaps because they pertain to another's suffering or the alleviation of that suffering, are often associated with a sense of heightened awareness of one's own condition and its moral implications," and so it's no wonder that Parks, like other great civil rights leaders, greatly inspired the young Wetherell.

The challenges faced by these heroes were the kinds of tests he could picture himself having to undergo one day. Watching war movies, he always wondered if he would crack under torture; watching Bull Connor's men go to work with their truncheons on the streets of Birmingham, he wondered if he would ever have the moral courage to march with the demonstrators who were taking the blows on their heads. He had nightmares, actual screaming nightmares, where he was being chased by the Klan like Andrew Goodman and his friends. He had moments, too, when he pictured himself standing on the steps of the Lincoln Memorial and addressing the huge crowd, like Martin Luther King, Jr.—and, morbidly shy now, he wondered whether he could find the courage to do even that.

This was only his imagination working—but that's precisely the point: The civil rights movement and heroes like Rosa Parks seized his imagination so forcibly that it would never be the same again.

Martin Luther King, Jr., admired Rosa Parks as he did few other people, writing "One can only understand the actions of Mrs. Parks when one realizes that eventually the cup of endurance runs over, and the human personality cries out, 'I can't take it any longer.' . . . No, she was not planted there by the NAACP; she was planted there by her sense of dignity and self-respect."

Yesterday, in glancing through the newspaper, I found that Johnnie Carr, age ninety-seven, had died the day before in Montgomery, Alabama. Much to my shame, the name was unknown to me, though she had been one of Rosa Parks's best friends and closest allies, and herself one of the great unheralded leaders of the civil rights movement. She succeeded Martin Luther King, Jr., as president of the Montgomery Improvement Association, and held that position until the day she died.

"Johnnie Carr is one of the three major icons of the civil rights movement: Martin Luther King, Jr., Rosa Parks, and Johnnie Carr," said Morris Dees, cofounder of the Southern Poverty Law Center. "I think ultimately, when the final history books are written, she'll be one of the few people remembered by name."

Reading about her brought it all back again—how much I had admired all of these activists, and the changes their courage had brought about. In a mood, I went downstairs to dig out an old Pete Seeger record, a live concert recording made in June of 1963 at Carnegie Hall. I played both sides, but cued up the last song three consecutive times: "We Shall Overcome," the famous civil rights anthem which Seeger himself had put together from several strands. Toward the end, he stops singing for a moment, but keeps strumming the solemn, hypnotic rhythm on his twelve-string, saying, "The best verse was made up in Montgomery, Alabama. It says *We are not afraid.* And here you and I up here, like every human in the world, we have been afraid—but you still sing it. *We are not afraid. We are not afraid.*"

A badly needed shot of Seeger, then a restorative chaser of Thoreau:

> Why is not the government more apt to anticipate and provide for reform? Why does it not cherish its wise minority? Why does it not encourage its citizens to be on the alert to point out its faults, and do better than it would have them? Why does it always crucify Christ, excommunicate Copernicus and Luther, and pronounce Washington and Franklin rebels? . . . I wish my countrymen to consider that, whatever the human law may be, neither an individual nor a nation can ever commit the least act of injustice against the obscurest individual without having to pay a penalty . . . I walk toward one of our ponds, but what signifies the beauty of nature when men are base? We walk to lakes to see our serenity reflected in them; when we are not

serene, we go not to them. Who can be serene in a country where both the rulers and the ruled are without principle?

I did not send to you for advice, but to announce that I am to speak.

PART TWO

The Golden Age of Admiration

PIERRE BEZUKHOV

If you plotted a person's life span out on a graph, superimposed over it a chart of their admirations, a bulge would jump out at you from the teenage years, where the admirations would be piled in an overflowing black kettle, as if the numerals fourteen, fifteen, and sixteen had the power to cook up heroes on their own. The demographics of admiration favor teenagers all the way, and you don't have to dig very deep into evolutionary genetics to speculate on why this is so. Young cavemen and cavewomen must have learned many of life's lessons through osmosis, as young people do now, and yet, when they came of age, they had to make explicit decisions about who, among the clan's leaders, they must respect, learn from, and follow—and so the admiring gene in teenagers, many millennia later, is still tuned to a fine and discriminating pitch.

In looking back on my own chart, I can see this bulge—this autobiography of admiration could limit itself to my sixteenth summer and still be a longish book. And for a chapter or two more, it will linger on that point, when, via admiration, I went from being a young boy I hardly recognize now to being someone who, at least in rough approximation, is the same one typing these words.

And with that change, it's time to say farewell to the third-person construction that has enabled me to write of the boy I once was as the distant character he so often seems. Henry Adams (whom I admire) is the one who invented this way of writing of yourself, though Adams runs with it all the way through his *Education*, not just when he's writing of his youth. Adams was good at admiration, and he started young by worshipping Charles Sumner, the famous Massachusetts senator in the years just before the Civil War:

> His superiority was real and incontestable; he was the classic ornament of the anti-slavery party; their pride in him was unbounded and their admiration outspoken. The boy Henry worshipped him, and if he ever regarded any older man as a personal friend, it was Mr. Sumner. The only fault of such a model was its superiority which defied imitation. To the twelve-year-old boy, Mr. Sumner was a different order—heroic.

Adams's third-person "Adams" is one of the most compelling autobiographical characters we have, but in this lesser "education," the third-person Wetherell has served us long enough. By sixteen, my heroes had carried me close enough to the person I became to write about them now with comfortable familiarity, and the only point to keep in mind is that it was these admirations themselves that formed the bridge, and all young Wetherell had to do was cross over it to become, for lack of a better word, *me*.

It's a mild July evening in 1805, and Russia's intellectual, artistic, and military elite are invited to a soiree at the elegant townhouse of Anna Pavlovna Scherer, the Tsarina's favorite lady-in-waiting. The partygoers include Prince Vasili Kuragin, "a man of high rank and importance"; his daughter Helene, known universally as *La Belle Helene*; Prince Andrew Bolonski, a rich landowner and natural-born leader of men who is on his way to Austria to become aide-de-camp to General Kutuzov in the new war against France; his pregnant wife, Princess Bolonski, *la femme la plus seduisante de Petersbourg,* yet, to her husband, a tiresome bore.

Arriving late is a "stout, heavily built young man with close-cropped hair, spectacles, the light-colored breeches fashionable at the time, a very high ruffle and a brown dress coat." His expression is "shy, but observant and natural, an expression which distinguished him from everyone else in that drawing room," and which is given added emphasis by the fact he is the biggest, burliest, clumsiest man there.

This earnest, bashful, argumentative young man is Pierre Bezukhov, the illegitimate son of Count Bezukhov, "a well-known grandee of Catherine's time who now lay dying in Moscow." Having just returned from a long stay abroad, anxious to learn more about the issues of the day, Pierre circulates from guest to guest, knowing that "all the intellectual lights of Petersburg were gathered there, and, like a child in a toy shop, he did not know which way to look, afraid of missing any clever conversation that was to be heard."

This goes badly, at least at first; when he hears everyone berating Napoleon, his hero, he can't hold himself back, but launches into a defense of the Emperor's policies that, bordering on treason, leaves everyone aghast. Prince Andrew is the only one who listens to him with tolerant sympathy—obviously, a great friendship is being forged—and no one is unhappy when Pierre turns abruptly to go.

Again, this is July 1805. And of all the men and women alive in Russia then, the boyars, peasants, generals, serfs, artisans, emperors, tradesmen, ladies-in-waiting, princes, servants, and anonymous millions, the names of only seven or eight are still alive today, 200 years later—and these are not people who were ever alive at all, but made-up people, Pierre Bezukhov and his friends, who, because they *are* made up, made up so brilliantly, will live quite literally forever.

Any young person who finds his way to *War and Peace* will probably share their best qualities with Pierre Bezukhov or they wouldn't have ventured into Tolstoy in the first place. There are so many great characters in the novel—the well-meaning, foolish Count Rostov; his daughter Natasha, the most vibrantly imagined young girl in all of literature; the dashing, truly gallant Prince Andrew, and his patient, long-suffering sister, Princess Mary; the murderously nihilistic, splendidly brave Dolokhov, and his existential counterpart, the wondrously sweet, splendidly brave Denisov . . . So many great characters that any one of them could be the central character, and *War and Peace* would still be a masterpiece.

And yet, for me, on the first reading when I was sixteen, Pierre stole the show. How could it be otherwise? I was husky like Pierre, I wore glasses like Pierre, I was shy, I was serious, already asking big questions of the world, without—until I read *War and Peace*—getting much in the way of answers.

I identified with him right from that first entrance at Anna Scherer's soiree, and my identification only deepened as his adventures went on. Tolstoy (who put much of himself into Pierre) has a marvelous way of constantly surprising us, giving the feeling that life with all its unpredictability and contradiction is in charge of his characters, not a novelist pulling the strings. Even as a teenager, I was a good-enough reader to sense this, and, rather than rooting for the book to go in the direction I wanted it to, like I usually did, I allowed the novel's life to work on my imagination with total patience and trust.

Pierre is at the heart of most of these surprises. Awkward, homely, the butt of jokes, he suddenly becomes the most desirable bachelor in Petersburg when his father dies, leaving him a fortune. He is manipulated into a marriage with *La Belle Helene;* then, when she flirts with Dolokhov, he challenges this notorious duelist to a duel—and, never having shot a pistol before, and terribly nearsighted, he ends up winning by shooting Dolokhov first.

The surprises, the contradictions, never stop. Pierre, searching for others who share his idealism, joins the Masons, but soon becomes disenchanted with their empty philosophy and cronyism. He tries giving away his fortune, but finds there are too many obstacles; he devotes himself to riotous living, then wants to kill himself from remorse. He witnesses the decisive Battle of Borodino, understands for the first time the horror of war, stumbles around a burning Moscow, convinced he's destined to assassinate Napoleon, his former hero, and then, when the French capture him and drag him along on their terrible retreat, he is befriended by a peasant named Platon Karataev, the last of the novel's great characters, who, through his simple, down-to-earth philosophy, gives Pierre the strength to endure his ordeal.

Pierre's greatest surprise struck me right in the heart. This clumsy, nearsighted version of myself falls in love with Natasha Rostov, and worships her from afar while her tragic love for Prince Andrew plays out. Just before the battles of 1812 break out, he goes to her house in Moscow to comfort her when it becomes definite that, thanks to her mad infatuation with Anatole Kuragin, her engagement to Andrew is over:

She began to cry and a still greater sense of pity, tenderness and love welled up in Pierre. He felt the tears trickle under his spectacles and hoped they would not be noticed.

"We won't speak of it, my dear—I'll tell him everything, but one thing I beg of you, consider me your friend and if you want help, advice or simply to open your heart to someone—not now, but when your mind is clearer—think of me!" He took her hand and kissed it. "I shall be happy if it's in my power. . . ."

Pierre grew confused.

"Don't speak to me like that, I am not worth it. All is over for me!" exclaimed Natasha and turned to leave the room, but Pierre held her hand.

"All over?" he repeated. "If I were not myself, but the handsomest, cleverest, and best man in the world, and were free, I would this moment ask on my knees for your hand and your love!"

Six hundred more pages' worth of adventures and ordeals await both of them before Pierre declares his love again—and finds that Natasha loves him. The entire novel, with its sweep of history, its intertwined destinies, its surprises of fate, has been working toward this point all along: the tremendous moment when Pierre finally gives up his long struggle for the meaning of life and finds, at last, acceptance:

The happiness before him appeared so inconceivable that if only he could attain it, it would be the end of all things. Everything ended with that . . . A joyful, unexpected frenzy, of which he had thought himself incapable, possessed him. The whole meaning of life—not for him alone but for the whole world—seemed to him centered in his love and the possibility of being loved by her . . . Often in afterlife Pierre recalled this period of blissful insanity. All the views he formed of men and circumstances at this time remained true for him always . . . Pierre's insanity consisted in not waiting, as he used to, to discover personal attributes which he termed "good qualities" in people before loving them; his heart was now overflowing with love, and by loving people without cause he discovered indubitable causes for loving them.

It's in this passage that we finally understand why Pierre is so admirable. Almost alone of fiction's great characters, he allows life to teach him its lessons, not only via hard living and the trials of existence everyone goes through, but by a wholehearted and heroic quest—and comes out of the journey, not cynical, not beaten, but sweeter, wholer, more charitable than before, the true hero of the greatest novel ever written, as admirable a man as we have an account of, and every reader's best friend.

I first read *War and Peace* at our summer house by the lake, my wannabe Walden. This was prime reading terrain—a small, slant-roofed bedroom with an extra bed I could pile library books on, and a fieldstone porch shaded by birches where I could read late into the evening, swatting at bugs. Our summers there provided the "quiet zone" any deeper reader needs apart from the world, especially a teenager who already sensed his life would somehow be caught up with books. It was on that porch where I read the above scene, cried my eyes out from happiness, then raced through the "First Epilogue," which, with its update on what happens to the main characters in later life, gives an almost overpowering sense of the flow of generations and the bittersweet passage of time.

War and Peace, the edition I first read, still owns a proud place in my bookcase, and I've just gone over to take it down. It's battered now—the spine in tatters, the cover flaking—but it's no more battered than it should be, seeing how it was published in 1942 during another great war.

I've read it once every five or six years since that first time (and remember watching a remarkable BBC version starring a young Anthony Hopkins as Pierre). As for Tolstoy himself, I respect him, of course, more the writer than the man. The man, if you read Troyat's biography, comes cluttered with too many relatives, too many disciples whose names mean nothing to us now—and then there's all that marital discord, which makes you want to turn away in embarrassment the way you do when your parents argue. Still, there is a stubborn, questing quality in Tolstoy as there is in Pierre, and you can't help but admire him when, on his deathbed, the famous old man runs away from Yasnaya Polyana and embarks on a final pilgrimage, only to die at the small railway station of Astapovo, beloved by everyone and universally mourned.

Reading Tolstoy led me, via a Dostoevsky detour and a Turgenev roundabout, to Chekhov, who turned out to be the writer I still admire most as a man. So it's appropriate to quote Chekhov on Tolstoy's influence, in words that, in our master-less age, seem poignantly nostalgic:

> I fear Tolstoy's death. His death would leave a large empty space in my life. First, I have loved no man the way I have loved him. I am not a believer, but of all the beliefs I consider his the closest to mine and most suitable to me. Second, when literature has a Tolstoy it's easy and gratifying to be a writer. Even if you are aware that you have never accomplished anything, and are still not accomplishing anything, you don't feel so bad, because Tolstoy accomplished enough for everyone.

ARTHUR FIEDLER

Before lip-syncing or playing air guitar there was air-conducting—but was I the last American teenager ever to do this? I would face the stereo in my room, cue up some Boston Pops or New York Philharmonic, Tchaikovsky probably, the "1812 Overture" or "March Slav." I'd listen to most of it on my bed with my eyes closed, but by the end I'd be on my feet, waving my arms about like I'd seen conductors do on television, cueing in the drums and the cannon, urging on the violins, supremely conscious not only of my orchestra—strings and woodwinds on the left, brass and percussion on the right—but of the elegant audience watching at my back. Showtime! I danced for them, or at least my arms and shoulders did, and I threw in all sorts of grimaces and scowls for emphasis.

And yet, withal, what I was most aware of was the overwhelming power of the music there in front of me, the way it caught my hearing in its torrent, tumbled my senses over, swept me along. I had taken piano lessons when I was younger, trumpet lessons, too, but the only thing they taught me was that I had absolutely no talent for making music; no, my talent was for music *appreciation*, and music appreciation, I now discovered, was going to play an increasingly larger role in my life.

It's possible that somewhere on this vast continent a sixteen-year-old boy or girl still air-conducts Tchaikovsky in the privacy of their room. But it's impossible to think of this being just a random, run-of-the-mill teenager who has found their way to classical music with an encouraging nudge from mass culture. Those helpful nudges no longer exist. Yes, there are specialists, teenagers whose parents persuade them to take up the violin early and find their way to classical music via this means, maybe even dream of becoming a conductor, but the ordinary teenager, never having heard classical music on his parents' CD player, never having heard it on the radio, never having heard it talked about in school, will, when they hear the name Tchaikovsky, either shrug in total incomprehension or make a face and say "Classical? Ughh!"

During my teenage years, or at least the pre-Beatles ones, popular culture still respected classical music. You could make a joke about someone waving their arms about "like a regular Toscanini" and everyone would get it; you could take a taxi in Manhattan and hear the cabbie talk about "Lenny" and know that he meant Leonard Bernstein. Leopold Stokowski, Herbert von Karajan, even Eugene Ormandy—the great conductors weren't quite pop stars, but the kind of respected, dignified figures everyone admired before pop stars dumbed things down.

Even a kid left at home before a TV set could stumble accidentally upon classical music, and I don't mean on the PBS channels (which, in any case, didn't exist yet). I remember a show that was on Saturday mornings (was it called *Odyssey*?) where the NBC Symphony Orchestra would play, or Metropolitan Opera stars would come on to sing the final trio from *Faust*. Classical music was taken seriously, and even Liberace, that mincing showman, felt it necessary to take on the trappings of a classical pianist in order to get across his kitsch.

Public schools, at least those near major cities, felt it important to expose students to classical music, and as a requirement, not just an elective. The music teacher in my grade school was an imposing, heavily rouged woman called Dr. Plinkavich. I don't know if the "doctor" was honorary or real, but she spoke with a thick foreign accent, and she may have been a distinguished wartime refugee. What I do remember is that she was so exotic, dignified, and self-possessed that even the rowdiest boys wouldn't make a peep in her class.

Dr. Plinkavich had a specialty: She wrote children's versions of the great operas and had her classes perform them in the school's auditorium. In fifth grade, it was *La Bohème*, and with only a chorus part myself, I fell in love with the Musetta, Elaine Houseman, who all the boys had crushes on, not just me; when she sang Musetta's aria ("Day after day, when I go strolling down the avenue, admiring glances follow me"), I nearly swooned from unrequited crush-dom.

In sixth grade, Dr. Plinkavich changed things slightly and had us perform a play based on the life of Johann Sebastian Bach. I had a minor but significant role as Bach's cruel stepfather, who, by forcing him to compose music by candlelight as a boy, eventually made him go blind. It was my first introduction to Bach—and what public school sixth-grader learns about Bach today? The other significant thing was my having to wear lederhosen as part of my costume; I was what in those days was termed "husky," and, terribly shy, I'd never worn shorts in public before, so my few bare-legged moments on stage used up every ounce of courage I had.

It was nice of the culture to do this for me—help make music a lifelong passion—but it wasn't going to do it for many others. I can pin down the precise moment and place that teaching young people about classical music totally fell apart: Mr. Miller's music appreciation class at Garden City Middle School on suburban Long Island, circa 1964. Mr. Miller was the personification of every incompetent, overmatched teacher who ever lived. (It would be interesting to spin time backwards and learn, through what failures and cock-ups, he found himself in front of our class.) "Harried" is the adjective that seemed draped around him in an even shabbier suit than his normal one; his black glasses slid down his greasy nose, and his attempts at being funny, which were never funny, were always followed by spasms of anger where he lashed out at everyone in sight.

Still, he tried. I remember one exercise he had us do: listening to Smetana's "Moldau" with our eyes closed, then, before the music finished, writing down our impressions of what the music suggested or conveyed. (I wrote about a flowing river, which was of course exactly what he wanted.) He may have repeated the exercise with the Largo from Dvorak's New World Symphony, so, thanks to him, I'd learned the names of at least two new composers.

That classical music is one of Western civilization's greatest adornments is not something the rest of the class fully appreciated. They had more earthly concerns, i.e., a girl named Tony who sat in the middle row of the risers that rose backwards from the blackboard. While the music was playing and we were supposed to have our eyes closed (Mr. Miller, leading by example, closed his own eyes and hummed), Tony, holding her spiral-bound notebook coyly at chest level, would unbutton her sweater, then her blouse, letting the boys on either side have a good long peek.

I sometimes wonder about this now—whether there are any late-middle-aged men in this country, graduates of this class, who, happening to hear Smetana on the radio, feel an inexplicable erotic charge. Me, I was too shy to ever peek at Tony myself; whenever I hear Smetana now, I still think of rivers, rushing rivers.

So, I was born just in time—a year or two later, and I would have grown up without any exposure to classical music whatsoever. I heard just enough in school to get me sufficiently interested to pursue it on my own, and inevitably this led me to the recordings of Arthur Fiedler and the Boston Pops.

It could have been the word itself that first drew me to them— "Pops"—with a whole train of pleasant associations it pulled down my cognitive tracks. Pop goes the weasel, soda pop, ice cream pops, pop as in Grandpop—it was a bright and happy word, so it was no wonder that the music the "Pops" played was lively and bouncy. The first album I found was a live recording of one of their Symphony Hall concerts, with the usual Pops mix—an overture, the "Pope and Peasant," then Leroy Anderson's "The Typewriter," complete with key taps and margin bells and carriage returns, then a slightly more serious work,

Grofé's "Grand Canyon Suite" (those clip-clopping mules!), followed, as dessert, by symphonic arrangements of the latest Beatles hits. It was a baby step toward "real" classical music, but it gave me a feel for strings, brass, and percussion that formed a foundation my growing sophistication could slowly build on.

As for Arthur Fiedler himself, I never learned much about him, other than that he looked like not only a great conductor, but an affable, impish one as well. (And half-crocked, in a genial way; his daughter would one day write a biography detailing his battles with alcoholism.) His rotund, roly-poly frame; his distinguished, Toscanini-ish white mustache; the brisk, businesslike arms and hands. He used all of these to convey an amiable kind of authoritarianism that went down perfectly with the music, so he neither seemed to condescend to it nor treat it as anything profound. RCA, his record label, tried making him seem more like a regular Joe than apparently he really was, posing him on album covers in a fire chief's helmet or an Indian war bonnet or a Red Sox cap, packaging him as a middlebrow good sport.

But all credit to him. I can't be the only person my age who first fell in love with classical music thanks to Arthur Fiedler and the Boston Pops.

Leonard Bernstein led me up the next rung of the classical music ladder, with an assist from Peter Ilyich Tchaikovsky. Bernstein was then at the height of his fame and influence, having composed the remarkable score to *West Side Story*, and having turned the New York Philharmonic into the most highly regarded orchestra in the world. He was also famous for his young persons' concerts on television, where, with a perfect combination of erudition, humor, and charm, he would explain to young viewers how an orchestra went about creating its sounds.

I recognized his name, recognized the New York Philharmonic "brand," and so his were the records I looked for—mostly Tchaikovsky, and mostly the obvious ones, "Swan Lake" or the "1812 Overture," complete with cannons, muskets, and bells. Tchaikovsky's sumptuous, youthfully passionate Romantic sound probably remains the best, most seductive means classical music has to snare a young person's interest, and my favorite Tchaikovsky was exactly what you would expect it to be: "The Nutcracker Suite."

I had a crush on a girl named Barbara Collier (well, more than a crush—a chaste, strictly-from-the-distance first love) who sat in front of me in Spanish. The unrequited stirrings this left in me were perfectly matched by Tchaikovsky's music, particularly the final waltz, which I would play over and over again in my room, while I pictured myself—shades of Tolstoy!—sweeping across a ballroom with Barbara Collier in my arms. Funny, touching, poignant—but much more important than that, too, and those fantasy moments listening to Tchaikovsky helped me decide (instinctively, without putting it into words) that what I wanted to do in life was to somehow dwell in the place where inexpressible yearning met overmastering beauty and created art.

Music took me there, even more impetuously than books. Listening to classical radio, WNCN in New York or WQXR, sophisticated up my tastes, and I began recognizing certain styles as belonging to certain composers or particular eras. I began paying attention to the performers' names, learned that Arthur Rubinstein was a pianist, Nathan Milstein a violinist, Pablo Casals a cellist. I searched through the record bins at A & S's, read the backs of the albums to learn more, thought long and hard before spending my $4.95, and then stacked them up in my bedroom until I had a respectable pile. I played them on the stereo and started in with my air-conducting. I knew not a single person who liked classical music or could talk about it with me; right from the start, this was a passion pursued as solo as it gets.

There was one more vital step to be made in this line, something that germinated now, but didn't really flower until several years later. As with so many admirations, it came to me first over the radio. Late Sunday night, awake in my darkened room, fiddling with the FM dial, I brushed against a station in New Jersey playing some stirring, passionate classical music I didn't recognize. I flopped back on my bed to listen—and was surprised when, a few bars later, the orchestra was joined by voices, three of them, one high female, one lower female, one deep male, singing so beautifully it was as if they were in the room with me. Opera! I remembered sixth grade and Dr. Plinkavich—and while a year earlier I would have made a face, jumped up, and tuned elsewhere, I stayed where I was on the bed, letting the sound wash over me, not caring that it was Italian and I didn't understand a single word.

I didn't *have* to understand. I let the emotion pour through my ears toward my heart the way I did when listening to "The Nutcracker"—and so, in virtually the first moment I ever listened to it, I "got" opera's secret. Where this would lead me, who it would lead me to, will be an important part of this memoir—but for now, it's just this serendipitous but perfectly timed moment in my room that's worth recording . . . the magical night when so many future admirations were first conceived.

ROBERT FROST

I discovered poetry much the same way I discovered classical music. There was at least a token attempt made to teach us about it in school (like everyone in my generation, I was forced to memorize Noyes's "The Highwayman"), and the culture still gave it just enough prominence—though it wouldn't much longer—that a certain amount just floated in the air where any young person, if they were so inclined, could grab it and run. This was the heyday of Robert Frost, one of the few public poets the country at large had ever honored, and certainly the last. He had read "The Gift Outright" at Kennedy's inauguration, and his wise, craggy New England visage, his handsome shock of white hair, seemed the perfect leavening to Kennedy's youthful energy and charisma.

Inevitable, that I should find my way to his poems. Having a summer house in Connecticut made me feel like a native New Englander (we had white birches galore, and if I searched hard in the second-growth woods, I could find the moss-covered bulges of old stone walls), and, with a mother who grew up on a farm during the Great Depression, I had sympathy for Frost's characters, alone and forgotten in a landscape that was emptying out. And Frost's poems, with their surface simplicity hiding unexpected depths, are perfect for a young person to cut his or her poetic teeth on. I found Caedmon recordings of Frost reading his favorites; he didn't read poems like I was used to hearing them read, as rhymes that came in a bouncy and repetitive rhythm, but more like they were stories, with a beat, a lilt, that was unlike anything I'd heard and uniquely his.

(In the history of admiration, the old Caedmon record company deserves thanks, since no one else was recording the great writers thirty years before books on tape were introduced. I remember listening to Dylan Thomas read, not just "A Child's Christmas in Wales," but his marvelous and overlooked short stories. No other male ever had a more hypnotic and beautiful voice. I also remember listening to Eudora Welty read "Why I Live at the P.O." in her ladylike and ironic Southern drawl.)

The first Frost poem I fell in love with was, of course, "Stopping by Woods on a Snowy Evening." I'd had that brief childhood fling with Tom Dooley, the muscular missionary, and one of his books was called *Miles to Go Before I Sleep*—and so I was delighted to find I already knew the poem's punch line. In eighth grade, we had to memorize a poem and recite it before the class; not only did I choose Frost's show-piece, but I arranged with a pal that when I got to the last stanza, he, standing behind the curtain on a ladder (we recited on stage), would drop handfuls of plastic snow over me—to wild applause and the teacher's A.

At a nearby discount store, thrown into the mass grave of a half-price bin, I found *The Complete Poems of Robert Frost*, the 1949 edition, which still holds a place in the bookcase at my back. The contents page has pencil checks by all my favorites: "The Death of the Hired Man," "My November Guest," "The Code," "The Road Not Taken," "Birches," "New Hampshire," "The Need of being Versed in Country Things," and "Canis Major."

Frost had a tragic sense of life in general and New England life in particular, and that's probably what I was responding to, once I got past the charm of old stone walls, swinging birches, and the dancing Hyla Brook. This was the pattern I followed in finding my way to other favorite poets—being captured by the surface, their subject matter, then finding deeper reasons to explore further. I read Elizabeth Bishop because she had a poem about a fish; Marianne Moore because she wrote about the Brooklyn Dodgers; Edwin Arlington Robinson because he wrote "Richard Cory," who Simon and Garfunkel had a song about; Edna St. Vincent Millay, because she wrote about Maine and even Connecticut.

Millay became a real favorite, and I ranked her just below Frost. I memorized the first few stanzas of "Renascence," the poem that won her fame as a teenager, and I still think it's a remarkable poem, capturing with incredible passion the bittersweet, heart-stopping beauty of life, or at least the beauty a young person is so sensitive to it nearly chokes them. "All I could see from where I stood," it starts, with such deceptive simplicity, "Was three long mountains and a wood . . ." and then, in a few more lines, you're plunged almost despite yourself straight into infinity.

I've never quite been able to decide why my passion for poetry, so intense for four or five years, didn't capture me for good. It may have been crowded out between music on the melodic side and prose on the rhythmic side. (All good prose, I was discovering, had a cadence and beat, and, for whatever reason, it captured me more than poetry's did.) While it lasted, though, my love of poetry was deep and inspiring, or why else, fifty years later, can I still recite so many poems by heart?

Here's a short one I memorized when I was sixteen or seventeen— not a Frost, but a poem called "The Cold Meteorite" by William Reed Huntington, a prescient warning to the cold, priggish young man I was in danger of becoming:

Far better tis to die the death that flashes gladness, than alone,

In frigid dignity, to live on high;
Better in burning sacrifice be thrown
Against the world to perish, than the sky to circle endlessly, a barren stone.

As for Frost the man, or as a sage to look up to, he falls a little short. His friend Lawrance Thompson did him no favors when he wrote a famously unflattering biography, which absolutely shocked those who thought he actually was the wise, tranquil New England farmer he resembled. Betrayals, failures, suicides—his family life was horrific, and it's not much fun reading about his selfish dedication to his art, even if, from poetry's point of view, it was entirely admirable. He had a big ego, and that gets in the way, too. Norman Mailer, who should know, wrote that "Frost, in his later years, was dependably as pleased with himself as any American author has ever been. Indeed, Robert Frost's infatuation with Robert Frost may be the American romance of the century."

Frost, for all his faults, was one of those who got me started writing juvenile poetry, and so, got me started writing, period. I was never very serious about my poems—I wrote them in idle moments under the birches on our summer house lawn—and most of them were about animals or lakes, or, yes, birches. As with my air-conducting Tchaikovsky, it was my infant attempt to be part of it all. The moment I finished them I forgot them—and yet the impulse to write something down, anything down, only grew stronger.

Admiration 101

BERTRAND RUSSELL

I'm always jealous when I hear someone refer to their college years as the most stimulating experience of their lives. They remember, these lucky grads do, being exposed for the first time to history's great thinkers; they remember professors who became their mentors, helped point them down the intellectual path they then followed for the rest of their careers.

My own college experience was so bland and forgettable it's hard to toss more than four or five sentences toward it. I learned in my late teens that I was a born autodidact; "self-educated" is a label I'm as proud of as anyone who boasts of being a Yale or Michigan grad. You don't become self-educated within the very corridors of establishment education without feeling like a rebel, which both linked me to my peers (I was far from the only rebellious twenty-year-old in 1968), and separated me from them (I was such a rebel I rebelled from rebellion).

In short, I went to college because it was expected of me, because my friends went, because it kept me out of the draft. It did little more than that; when it came to preparing me for my future, a young man who knew he was born to write, it taught me nothing. But if you discount all this, scrape away the autodidactic chip which sat on my shoulder, my late teens and early twenties were good years when it came to admiration. My hunger for learning was as great as anyone's who thrived in the academic setting, and I needed and found mentors just like they did.

The first and most important of these was Bertrand Russell. I found him entirely on my own, reading an excerpt from his famous essay,

"A Free Man's Worship," in, of all things, a book about rural Maine. I did *not* find his work in college, significantly enough; I majored in philosophy, so surely my professors all knew about him, but I don't remember his name ever being mentioned, except briefly in my ethics class on the day he died.

In 1940, notoriously, Russell had been prevented from taking a teaching post at City College of New York by a vicious right-wing smear campaign, which accused him of immorality and "freethinking." ("A professor of paganism," he was called by the Catholic Church and their allies at the tabloids and city hall. "A desiccated, divorced, decadent advocate of sexual promiscuity, an ape of genius, the devil's minister to men.") The case reminded more than a few people of how Athens had turned on Socrates precisely because he was so incorruptible and virtuous. Was it lingering timidity over this affair that even in 1967 kept my professors from assigning his books? Russell was exactly the kind of thinker who a young person *should* read in college, and it says everything about my academic experience that I had to find him on my own.

It's nearly impossible to describe the role in the world Bertrand Russell once filled, since there is no one remotely like him today. Cross the intellectual authority of Stephen Hawking with the moral leadership of Nelson Mandela, add in the—but no; any hybrid comparison immediately falls apart.

British aristocrat. Theoretical mathematician. Epistemologist. Analytical philosopher. Popularizer of science. Education pioneer. Ethicist. Dissident. Savant. Winner of the Nobel Prize in Literature. Author of countless books ranging from *Principia Mathematica* to *The Conquest of Happiness*. Campaigner against nuclear weapons. Out-surviving all his critics, dying in 1970 at age ninety-eight . . . Russell's moral authority and intellectual influence were immense. In the '60s, he was famous (and/or notorious) for being one of the leaders of the Campaign for Nuclear Disarmament, and photos of a defiant, wizened Russell being carried off to jail by the bobbies after a sit-down demonstration in Trafalgar Square remains one of the most indelible images of the ban-the-bomb movement. "Remember your humanity and forget all the rest," is how he ended his famous plea for world peace in 1960 over the BBC, when nuclear war seemed so near—and who's to deny that his sane and passionate voice helped pull the world through those darkest Cold War days?

All the sadder, then, to find that Russell's name is all but forgotten today, at least by young people who could profit from him the most. His writing was always marked by a passionate rationalism, and whatever else our age is, it is *not* passionately rational. He was also a great believer in the inner freedom that comes from self-discipline, and this is not a message our hedonistic, self-entitled era wants to hear either. "The Stoic freedom is which freedom consists," Russell writes, "is found in the submission of our desires but not of our thoughts." We, of course, are of a generation that likes to submit our thoughts to all kinds of fetters and restrictions, and, in a petulant kind of over-compensation, give our desires total license to do anything they please. It's no wonder Russell is forgotten.

His most famous essay, the one I found first, is "A Free Man's Worship" from 1903. It's written in a lyrical, Romantic style that is entirely unlike the rest of his writings and yet the philosophy expressed there remained absolutely core. It's a courageous attempt by an atheist to show how mystery, wonder, tragedy, hope, love, and pity can be as deep a part of his or her approach to the world as it can be in anyone conventionally religious—nay, even deeper, since this kind of metaphysical reverence doesn't rely on ready-made, easy-to-digest mythology or dogma:

> In the spectacle of death, in the endurance of intolerable pain and in the irrevocableness of a vanished past, there is a sacredness, an overpowering awe, a feeling of the vastness, the depth, the inexhaustible mystery of existence, in which, by some strange marriage of pain, the sufferer is bound to the world by bonds of sorrow . . . The slave is doomed to worship Time and Fate and Death, because they are greater than anything he finds in himself, and because all his thoughts are of things which they devour. But, great as they are, to think of them greatly, to feel their passionate splendor, is greater still. To abandon the struggle for private happiness, to expel all eagerness of temporary desire, to burn with passion for eternal things—this is emancipation, and this is the free man's worship.

It's impossible to exaggerate the visceral effect this essay had on me. Brought up within a mild, Sunday school kind of religion, I'd had no trouble at eighteen breaking away from it entirely—or was this quite as easy as I'd thought? I had easily jettisoned the Sunday school part, the all-too-familiar Bible stories, and a creation myth I'd never really responded to, but, reading Russell, I realized that I still had deep feelings of reverence that had to be accounted for, though without a man-made god on top. Russell pointed me in the direction to look— toward a tradition far wider, older, and wiser than anything offered by Christianity.

I read the following passage from "A Free Man's Worship" over and over again, until, quite literally, it became a part of me, and powered my passionate, over-the-top love of literature, which, like a stubborn and foolish dodo, I still feel today. With Camus's equally powerful essay, "Create Dangerously," it formed the cornerstone of what became my budding artistic creed:

> Of all the arts, tragedy is the proudest, the most triumphant, for it builds its shining citadel in the very center of the enemy's country, on the very summit of his highest mountain; from its impregnable watchtowers, his camps and arsenals, his columns and forts are all revealed; within its walls the free life continues, while the legions of death and pain and despair, and all the servile captains of tyrant Fate, afford the burghers of that dauntless city new spectacles of beauty. Happy those sacred ramparts, thrice happy the dwellers on that all-seeing eminence. Honor to those brave warriors who, through countless ages of warfare, have preserved for us the priceless heritage of liberty and have kept undefiled by sacrilegious invaders the home of the unsubdued.

That's one of the lessons I learned from Russell: how a tragic view of life can bring the person who holds it, counterintuitively, the most happiness. (Russell: "It wasn't until I finally accepted how horrible life is that I was able to be happy.") His second, equally important lesson was in some respects completely the opposite: the virtues of cool, no-nonsense ratio- nalism. Russell, remember, was a professional philosopher, an analytical philosopher, which is to say one who devoted much of his career to exposing cant, hypocrisy, and what he disdainfully called "intellectual rubbish."

A touch of Russellian lucidity was just what I needed at that point in my life. My skepticism was very much a twenty-year-old's, depending more on instinct than on reason, and I needed grounding in logic and the history of ideas if the skepticism was going to supply me with anything more than an "attitude." At the same time, I had that literary Romanticism, which could have gone badly astray if it wasn't tethered to some solid intellectual discipline. How my contemporaries hated that word, *discipline*, particularly if it had *self* as a prefix, but I realized, thanks to Russell and Camus, that it was the path to all I wanted to accomplish.

Since I worshipped Russell, I read everything about his personal life I could find, especially his *Autobiography*, which had just been published. He knew everyone, in that clubby British way, so there's plenty on figures like Conrad, D. H. Lawrence, and Bernard Shaw; what's more surprising, for such a donnish-looking man, was that he had a dramatically turbulent love life, with many marriages and affairs. But unlike most heroes under close examination, he doesn't have feet of clay. "Three passions, simple but overwhelmingly strong, have governed my life," he wrote. "The longing for love, the search for knowledge, and unbearable pity for the suffering of mankind." And when you read about his life, these virtues are indeed what stand out.

Even now, writing here of all those I admired, my emotions do something special when I read again Russell's words. He was my college, my alma mater, or as near as I've got, so I guess it's the old school ties stirring. Russell himself wrote his own epitaph—wrote it several times, as it happened, since he lived to a great old age and continued writing almost until the end. His final summation, the last paragraph of his autobiography, is as fine a last word as courage can give us:

> Beneath all this load of failure I am still conscious of something that I feel to be victory. I may have conceived theoretical truth wrongly, but I was not wrong in thinking that there is such a thing, and that it deserves our allegiance. I may have thought the road to a world of free and happy human

beings shorter than it is proving to be, but I was not wrong in thinking that such a world is possible and that it is worthwhile to live with a view to bringing it nearer. I have lived in the pursuit of a vision, both personal and social. Personal: to care for what is noble, for what is beautiful, for what is gentle; to allow moments of insight to give wisdom in more mundane times. Social: to see in imagination the society that is to be created, where individuals grow freely, and where hate and greed and envy die because there is nothing to nourish them. These things I believe, and the world, for all its horrors, has left me unshaken.

WAYNE MORSE

I felt the undertow of the '60s, but not the decade's thunderous wave. More's the pity, I sometimes think. A tumultuous ride on the crest of history might not have been such a bad thing. Demonstrations where I got spat on, yet proudly kept marching. A rose stem I rammed down a National Guardsman's rifle barrel. Chicago cops I screamed "Pigs!" at while they beat me all to hell. Forty years later, these might be proud and pleasant memories to look back on, assuming I had kept faith with the idealism which prompted them, hadn't seen it turn to dust.

"I didn't want to be too radical when young," Robert Frost once wrote, "in fear that I would become too conservative when old," and something like this caution operated on me. While I sympathized with the demonstrations and protests, I never took part. My morbid shyness was primarily to blame; in my late teens and early twenties, I suffered from an almost total social paralysis, so I was unable to bring myself to go to dances or parties, let alone demonstrations involving thousands. Then, too, I was repelled by the radicals, felt too many were in it for their egos or to attract girls or because it was trendy; I also sensed, very dimly, that I was playing a deeper game when it came to idealism—that once I found my way in life, I would protest in a more stubborn, private, permanent way.

But still, the decade left its mark. I remember as a high school senior attending a seminar where the talk was all of Mario Savio and the Berkeley Free Speech Movement, which I had never heard of. This must have been 1966—still a bit early in what we think of as the '60s, at least on solidly bourgeois Long Island. I had a sense that something was happening out there in the country at large, but no one was tipping me off as to what, and the first time I remember encountering current history face-to-face was at the first college I attended, a small liberal arts college in Vermont, whose distinguished speaker series included on one Sunday evening the dissident senator from Oregon, Wayne Morse.

His talk was in the college chapel. A professor rambled on too long with an introduction, but covered the major points—how Morse, a brilliant legal scholar, had begun his political career as a Bob La Follette–style progressive Republican, then, finding the party lurching to the right, switched to the Democrats in 1952, earning himself a reputation as a maverick.

The maverick stood up now, walked quickly and spryly up to the pulpit. He looked like an angry, fired-up version of Captain Kangaroo—the white mustache was the only gentle thing about him. His black glasses seemed to project forthrightness and indignation over the audience in hot stereo beams; his hoarse voice cracked under the pressure of his outrage; he pointed and jabbed a finger, not just at us, but at the folks in the administration he was lambasting so thoroughly.

It was Vietnam he was talking about, and the longer he talked, the angrier he grew. Why, the president had lied to us about the whole damn thing, was lying to us now, his administration being little more than a pack of liars. American boys were dying, and what for? Just to prop up a corrupt regime that had no support from its own people? The domino theory was wrong, the Communist China connection was overstated, the Vietcong, at worst, were nationalist patriots we should be helping, not fighting. The Senate, his beloved Senate, was filled with cowards, the whole cringing pack. The only development that gave him hope was the student demonstrations that were springing up all across the country, and it would be a damn good thing if we started demonstrating right here in the beautiful Green Mountain State of Vermont.

"It is unconstitutional to send American boys to their deaths in South Vietnam. I don't know why we think, just because we're mighty, that we have the right to substitute might for right. And that's the American policy in Southeast Asia. It's just as unsound when we do it as when Russia does it. I do not intend to put the blood of this war on my hands."

Powerful stuff. Never before had I listened to a senator speak in person, and never before had I seen such a palpably good man so sincerely angry. As for Vietnam, I was firmly in the antiwar camp even before he spoke, and this went back a surprisingly long way. In late 1961, or early 1962, well before adults in America were talking about Vietnam, let alone thirteen-year-olds, I had an eighth-grade social studies teacher named Mr. Tipton, who, when it came time to teach us the formal rules of debate, chose as our topic "Should the U.S. Become More Involved in South Vietnam?"

I don't remember much about Mr. Tipton, though there was a rumor passed on by a hitchhiking classmate about empty vodka bottles rattling around the backseat of his car. He showed a prescience verging on genius, forcing his eighth-graders to focus on the one spot in the world that, even for draft evaders, would come to dominate our lives. By the luck of the draw, I was assigned to be on the dove-ish side of the question (though no one then talked of "doves" or "hawks"). I remember researching hard in the library, then arguing for the immediate withdrawal of the few hundred advisors we had over there at the time, arguing for this with real thirteen-year-old passion and heat.

(On the opposite side of the question was a tall, gentle-mannered boy named Phillip Sheridan, like the famous general—Phil, whose name, thirty years later, I found on the wall in Washington.)

So, thanks to Mr. Tipton's class, I was more than receptive to Senator Morse's arguments. And I wasn't the only one either. This was 1966, still a bit early in the antiwar movement, but his speech at our isolated college made real converts. Most of the freshmen men, fearing the draft, figuring they should at least go as officers, had enrolled in the college ROTC program (this was before anyone understood that being a lieutenant meant buying a ticket straight to Saigon). The day after Morse's speech, five men in my hall immediately resigned from ROTC—and a year later, ROTC had been banished from the campus. Morse was changing minds, all right. He joined the handful of other respected oldsters, like Dr. Spock and Robert Lowell, who young people my age were drawing inspiration from and learning to trust. Ken Kesey, the novelist "Merry Prankster," spoke for a lot of us when he said, "Morse was the *only* guy we had."

I kept my eye on Morse after that, and the drama of his brave, lonely dissent. He had been one of two senators to vote against the Tonkin Gulf Resolution, giving the president carte blanche to do what he wanted in Vietnam. Even William Fulbright, who turned so decisively against the war, voted with Johnson on Tonkin. (Historians now speculate that Morse, through inside sources at the Pentagon, knew the destroyer incident that provoked the resolution was entirely fabricated.) In retrospect, I admire Morse even more than I did then, since what I was witnessing on that high chapel pulpit was a sight that was to become rare in future years: the spectacle of a good angry man—that is, a man who was good and who was angry at the same time. Our national life would soon become dominated by men and women who were bad and angry, and to see virtuous anger would become a rare thing.

(Before seeing Morse, I'd seen an angry bad man in person: Lyndon Johnson. It was on a family trip to Washington in 1959 or 1960. We had taken a tour of the Capitol while the Senate was in session, and our guide, as we gathered around him in the chamber's balcony, pointed out to us the leader of the Senate, Lyndon Baines Johnson, standing there directly below us before his old elementary-school-like desk. We stared down at his balding head, and just at that moment, needing a page to carry a message, he slammed his fist hard and imperiously down on the desktop, until a timid page hurried over—a scene that made me think of Fagin summoning Oliver Twist. Often in those disastrous years ahead, with all that happened in that misbegotten war, I would remember a red-faced Johnson slamming his fist down on his desk, and *not* be surprised at anything he did.)

Morse died in 1974, a brave, angry, lonely figure right to the end. In the U.S. Senate, he left no heirs.

BERNIE GEOFFRION

College wouldn't be college without some frivolity, especially frivolity taken much too seriously. That's what college sports is all about, and though the colleges I attended must have had teams, I paid them zero attention. And yet I was crazy about a team those years, cared so much for their players that I lived and died with their results. It was my guilty pleasure, my break from too much introspection, the last transmogrified flicker of my childhood love for the Dodgers and Yankees—and, when it came to the mainstream of my admirations, a pleasant side channel that did me no harm.

I knew about the New York Rangers because, during high school, a friend had taken me to four or five of their games. This was the only National Hockey League of only six teams, and while the Rangers always finished last, they had some interesting players, including the stylish Andy Bathgate, the reliable Harry Howell, the phlegmatic goalie Gump Worsley (who we agreed looked exactly like his first name; whatever "gump" meant, that was him), the rough and tough "Leaping Lou" Fontinato, and, best of all, the slender, delicate Camille "The Eel" Henry. By flashing our high school identity cards we got into the old Madison Square Garden for 75 cents, which gave us seats in the highest section behind a pillar.

Those were the days when smoking was still permitted everywhere, and by the third period a dense nicotine haze would settle over the ice, creating the garish atmosphere you see in boxing movies of the '50s. (If you're tempted to compare the skills of today's athletes against those of that earlier generation, remember that Bill Russell, Wilt Chamberlain, and Bobby Hull played inside clouds of noxious secondhand smoke.) Every game I saw seemed to be against the Detroit Red Wings and their star, Gordie Howe; the games would be tight until the final period, when Howe, having played semi-bored up to this point, would gather in the puck at mid-ice, knock several terrified Rangers over with his elbow, glide in toward Worsley, flick his wrist, and score—though by then, from where we were sitting, we could hardly see the ice through the pall.

The Rangers did slightly better that year (1967), thanks to the inspirational play of Bernie Geoffrion. "Boom Boom" Geoffrion had been a star on the great Montreal Canadiens team of the '50s, and became a hero in French Canada after inventing the "slap shot," where you didn't flick your wrists to shoot a la Gordie Howe, but instead swung your stick with your shoulders like a golfer driving off a tee. "Boom Boom" came from the sound Geoffrion's incomparably hard, heavy shots made when they missed the net and hit the boards. The Boomer had been retired for at least three years before he came back to join the Rangers (ONE MORE BOOM OR BUST FOR THE BOOMER! ran the *Sports Illustrated* headline), and, once he forced his burly body back into shape, his leadership made a big difference in the team's fortunes.

When I transferred colleges back to New York, bored, I let myself become even more infatuated with the Rangers. In those days they practiced at a rink on Long Island not far from my home—a neighborhood ice rink, damp, shabby, and dark, not exactly a venue you would associate with a major league sports team, even then. But many of the players rented homes on the Island during the season, the rink was convenient, and no one else was using it on weekday mornings. The rink owners charged 50 cents to watch, and, with plenty of free time on my hands (I never studied), I would walk the two miles over to the rink, plop my quarters down, and take up a position behind one goal, where I was virtually taking part in the practice myself. Pucks would fly over the chicken wire and I would throw them back on the ice; sticks would break, be tossed over the boards, and I would collect them for souvenirs.

The Rangers had an engaging mix of personalities during those years, and, watching so close, I got to know them quite well. From the old days they still had Harry "The Horse" Howell, as handsome as ever, though his hair was now turning gray. Camille "The Eel" Henry still played, too, though he seemed even wanner now, as if an ulcer were eating him up inside. Younger teammates included Rod Gilbert, movie-star handsome, graceful, and swift; his childhood friend and line mate, Jean Ratelle, perhaps the smoothest player in the NHL; Donnie Marshall, who looked like a balding English teacher, and seemed far too sensitive to play professional hockey; Reggie "The Ruffian" Fleming, the team's enforcer, the kind of guy who's friendly enough to sit next to at a bar, as long as you avoid pissing him off; and Phil Goyette, another of those sensitive-looking, intelligent, oddly delicate players the Rangers seemed to favor those years.

In this group, the Boomer stood out just from the sheer happy force of his personality. He had charisma, the Boomer did, and it wasn't just from those slap shots. He liked to joke around with his teammates; you could tell they were thrilled when he deigned to tease them, and, if they all worked hard at their drills, Bernie seemed to agonize more openly, collapsing onto his knees in exhaustion, so you could see him fighting his limits and making no apologies that it hurt. I loved hearing him interviewed, with that unapologetic French-Canadian accent; listening to him pronounce the word "three" as "tree" was good preparation for me when, many years later, I married into a family of Quebecois. He had that fleshy, well-dined-and-proud-of-it look many of my in-laws would have—an endomorph, but a happy, passionate one, and when he scowled, he put as much force and intensity into it as he did his smiles.

As well as watching them practice that year, I managed to see maybe eight or nine of their games. These were at the new Madison Square Garden over on Eighth Avenue—antiseptic and cold, at least compared to the smoky den I remembered. Just as in the old days when I had watched Gordie Howe single-handedly destroy them, I now saw the Bruins' Bobby Orr disdainfully rip them to shreds. Orr's superiority was such that even someone who knew nothing about hockey could tell, watching him skate, that he was playing on an entirely different, higher plane. The Rangers, sad to say, never went very far in the playoffs; they were one of those teams everyone loves, but who forever disappoint.

But, for me, they helped at a difficult time. Rooting for them so fiercely helped make tolerable an increasingly intolerable situation: living at home, going to a college I hated, working menial jobs, totally cut off from any friends. Loneliness can descend so suddenly, so oppressively, almost anything that helps lift it becomes cherished, and if now, looking back, I have to be slightly embarrassed for having worshipped someone called "Boom Boom," the relief he and his teammates gave me was very real. While I was a kid, turning sports stars into heroes was an easy and innocent thing; as a young man, that admiration required a willing suspension of disbelief (watching the Rangers in practice, they were all so obviously just human)—but the Boomer had enough flash to help me pull this off. He played one more season for the Rangers, and then the legs he had pushed so hard finally gave out. I was saddened, a few years ago now, to read of his death, and not surprised at all to read that his passing caused all French Canada to genuinely mourn.

WILLA CATHER

College slowed my reading down only slightly. I don't remember spending much time in the college library—it seemed tainted by its proximity to the classrooms. The public library in my town was vine-covered and genteel, but, like the Ivy League schools it was meant to resemble, largely hollow once inside. I used interlibrary loan to get a card to the neighboring town's library, which, while drabber, had stacks upon stacks of books. I did my best to read them all, to the point where, when I think nostalgically back to my alma mater, I remember the Hempstead Public Library, give it all credit for what I've become.

One of the authors I found those years was Willa Cather. I had first heard of her in high school, where her famous story, "Neighbor Rosicky," was assigned in English. It was, and still is, a remarkable story. Very few writers have ever had Cather's gift for writing about happiness. Now, remembering her name as I browsed through the stacks, I went right to her masterpiece, *My Antonia*. It hit me hard, right from that first reading, and I still include it in my five favorite novels of all time. I cried when I finished reading it—not because it was sad, but because she put down on paper happiness, hope, and endurance so perfectly, capturing, in Russell's phrase, "the overmastering beauty of human existence"—and all this through the story of a simple, uneducated farm girl, Antonia Shimerda.

No American writer ever found a more perfect prose style to tell her story with. It's a lyrical style, but smart enough to know when to cut back to simplicity, so the imagination, the eye, is ballasted and sharpened by the living world.

Here the narrator, Jim Burden, remembers the way the endless, windswept Nebraska prairie looked to him as a boy: "Perhaps the glide of the long railway travel was still with me, for more than anything else I felt motion in the landscape; in the fresh, easy-blowing morning wind, and in the earth itself, as if the shaggy grass were a sort of loose hide, and underneath herds of wild buffalo were galloping, galloping."

No need for Cather to say, "Nebraska once had lots of buffalo"— in her prose, without any explicit mention, their ghosts still run. And that goes for the famous metaphor that brings Jim's boyhood to an end and launches him out into the world, rooted in the landscape as few people ever are. Jim and Antonia, with the vibrant "hired girls" everyone else in town looks down on, go out for a last picnic on the prairie:

> Presently we saw a curious thing. There were no clouds, the sun was going down in a limpid, gold-washed sky. Just as the lower edge of the red disk rested on the high fields against the horizon, a great black figure suddenly appeared on the face of the sun. We sprang to our feet, straining our eyes toward it. In a moment we realized what it was. On some upland farm, a plow had been left standing in the field. The sun was sinking just behind it. Magnified across the distance by the horizontal light, it stood out against the sun, was exactly contained within the circle of the disc; the handles, the tongue, the share—black against the molten red. There it was, heroic in size, a picture writing on the sun . . . Even while we whispered about it, our vision disappeared; the ball dropped and dropped until the red tip went beneath the earth. The fields below us were dark, the sky was growing pale, and that forgotten plow had sunk back to its own littleness somewhere on the prairie.

Which may just be the best-written passage in all of American literature. Cather herself, elsewhere in the book, underlines the moral of her own scene. "This is happiness: to be dissolved into something complete and great . . ." and the moral, not just of *My Antonia*, but of Cather's entire career.

Cather was one of the first writers I read in an entirely new way—not just for enjoyment, not just for the magic, but trying to understand *where* the magic came from, and how, through what tricks of technique or largeness of spirit, I might capture it myself. So, for instance, I paid special attention to the marvelous way Cather uses *My Antonia*'s minor characters, the care she takes in making them come alive. She seems to have been possessed of a special tenderness for almost everyone she writes about, even villains, and writes out of an empathy that lies at the center of her art.

My Antonia abounds in great minor characters. There are the two farmhands who take Jim under their wing, Jake Marpole and Otto Fuchs, foolish, naive, hardworking, and generous; Antonia's violin-playing father, Mr. Shimerda, who dies of homesickness for his native Bohemian woods; Mrs. Stevens, the very personification of sensible, no-nonsense neighborliness; the itinerant piano player, Blind d'Arnault, who, growing up a sightless young slave, gropes his way to his master's piano.

You get the sense, reading *My Antonia*, of a great talent coming fully into its own. Cather began her career writing muckraking journalism, and her first attempts at fiction were stilted and artificial. It was Sarah Orne Jewett, the Maine short story writer, who advised her to write of the landscape she knew best (I admire Jewett—another of those rare writers who can make happiness seem real), and, in *My Antonia*, this note of artistic homecoming is very explicit.

Here, Jim studies Virgil in college under the tutelage of his brilliant young professor, Gaston Cleric:

> I turned back to the beginning of the third book of the Georgics, which we had read in class that morning. *Primus ego in patrium mecum . . . deducam Musas.* "For I shall be the first, if I live, to bring the Muse into my country." Cleric had explained to us that *patria* here meant, not a nation or even a province, but the little rural neighborhood in the Minco where the poet was born. This was not a boast, but a hope, at once bold and devoutly humble, that he might bring the Muse to his father's fields, "sloping down to the river and the old beech trees with broken tops."

This dream inspires Jim—and clearly inspired Cather—to be the first to bring art to the rolling, empty prairie land where she grew up. For that matter, this dream inspired me, too, though it worried me considerably—how to bring the Muse to bear on Long Island's concrete ordinariness. (Impossible, I decided, and except for a short story or two, all my landscapes were eventually to be found elsewhere.)

On a shelf with my reference books is *Cyclopedia of World Authors*, published in 1958. Cather's entry is written by someone named Dayton Kohler, and it's a truthful, moving summary of her place in our literature, a "writer's writer" if there ever was one (I take pride in knowing that Cather, who knew and loved the New Hampshire hills, is buried not far from my home):

> Willa Cather was the last of a generation of writers who lived through the passing of the old frontier, who saw at first hand the regions of the homesteader transformed into a countryside of tidy farms and small towns; and she found in the primitive virtues of the pioneer experience her own values as an artist . . . Cather thought of the novel as an instrument of culture, not a vehicle for social reportage or character-mongering, and art worth a lifetime's effort and devotion. Her literary masters were the European craftsmen who she so greatly admired, but her own writing was American in subject and mood. Coming at the end of an era, she tried to recapture a past which was at once innocent and romantic and heroic. That was her aim and her achievement, and what she had to say she said with honesty and simplicity, with moral subtlety and stylistic evocation. Her fidelity to her vision of experience testifies to her integrity as a person and an artist.

Total Admiration

FREDRIC MARCH

I once shook hands with Laurence Olivier.

This would have been the summer of 1978 or '79, at the old Treadway Hotel on the waterfront in Newport, Rhode Island. After leaving college, I had a variety of jobs; my pattern was to work for a few months, save enough money to rent a cabin in the woods, quit my job, write until the cash ran out, and then find another job and start the cycle again.

This eventually led me to a job as tour director on bus tours of New England. My driver and I would load our tourists at the Waldorf in Manhattan, drive them to Cape Cod, ride the ferries with them out to Martha's Vineyard and Nantucket, zip up to Provincetown for a dune buggy ride and clambake, and then drive down to Newport for a tour of the grand mansions, the ones the robber barons built themselves on the craggy Atlantic headlands. It was a demanding job in the way adult babysitting can be demanding, but I took it seriously, and between the lavish tips and having no expenses, the money piled up fast, earning me seven months of freedom in which to write.

That's what brought me to the Newport Treadway on a hot June afternoon. I jumped off the bus, rushed into the lobby to get my group's room keys, counted through them to make sure I had everybody's, and was just turning to run back out again when one of the desk clerks I knew, an aspiring actor, called something after me.

"When you come back in I'll introduce you to Larry."

By Larry he meant Sir Laurence Olivier. What had brought him to the Treadway wasn't all that different than what had brought me—money, the pressing need for it. With all the honors his career had brought him, he'd never earned as much as his reputation warranted, and he had decided, now that he was old, to rake in some fat paychecks so as to leave something to his family. He made cameo appearances, campy and brilliant, in a whole range of otherwise-forgettable films, and the one he was filming now was a wretched mishmash called *The Betsy*. The production had come to Newport to use one of the Gilded Age mansions, and so here Olivier was, living on the top floor of the Treadway, largely invisible except for when he descended for the evening "shoot."

When I got my tourists settled, I came back to my friend at the front desk. "So, you're kidding, right?" I said.

"Nope. He comes down every day around five." A binging noise made us glance to where the elevator door slid open. "Larry? This is my friend, Walter Wetherell."

A split second before freezing entirely, I stuck out my hand. The man who stepped forward and took it was old, not quite wizened but heading in that direction, at least if you concentrated on his face. Around it, his head was marvelous, easily the most striking, dignified, bust-like head I'd ever seen on a human being—the face, so familiar, seemed somehow secondary compared to the overall effect created by his profile. Many actors, many men, can charm you through their eyes, but how many can seduce you through their phrenology? Olivier could. And there was nothing wrong with his eyes—the vibrant way they shone *compelled* admiration.

"Hello, hello," he said—I remember distinctly him saying that twice. For a second that he managed by sheer force of personality to make seem much longer, I and I alone was the focus of all Olivier's interest. There was something he wanted to ask my friend the desk clerk about, a problem with the air-conditioning (the Treadway, sad to say, was something of a dump), and then he was whisked away by the various people who must always have been waiting to whisk him away.

In writing of my admirations, I've been aware of an unwritten book that my memory is sketching on its own, a parallel account that explains why I *didn't* admire various admirable candidates everyone else my age fell for, and why there were certain occupations or fields from which I never drew any heroes whatsoever. Of these larger classes, the ones that would take the most explaining is films. I fell for film stars, but in an entirely conventional way, looking to them for entertainment, nothing deeper.

As for movies in general, it's hard to explain why they never captured me the way they did my fellow boomers. I remember coming out of *West Side Story* and being deeply moved (I was fourteen) by the choreographed rumbles and Bernstein's score. Then, later, seeing *Casablanca* for the first time, I was stirred to the depths of my surprisingly Romantic young soul. Other than those, I'd have a hard time remembering a movie that influenced me as much as even the most mediocre of novels I was then devouring. Film is a communal art, and perhaps I was already too much the loner to care for it deeply. Shy, going through an odd and difficult period without any friends, I never took dates to films, so movies for me never carried the erotic charge all my peers were greedily enjoying.

Never having fallen for films, I never dreamed of writing them. The only thing I knew about Hollywood was that Holden Caulfield's brother worked there in *The Catcher in the Rye*, and right in the novel's first paragraph, J. D. Salinger (whom I admired) expressly warns would-be writers of ever going near the place:

> My brother D.B. is in Hollywood. He's got a lot of dough now. He didn't use to.
>
> He wrote this terrific book of short stories, *The Secret Goldfish*, in case you never heard of him. The best one in it was "The Secret Goldfish." It was about this little kid that wouldn't let anybody look at his goldfish because he'd bought it with his own money. It killed me. Now he's out in Hollywood, D.B. being a prostitute. If there's one thing I hate, it's movies. Don't even mention them to me.

Me, I wanted to write "The Secret Goldfish," not *The Graduate* or even *Casablanca*. In pursuit of this goal, I picked October to quit my latest job (Macy's, sporting goods and men's suits), packed my Volkswagen with my few belongings, and moved up to my parents' empty summer house by a Connecticut lake. My heroes were with me all the way on this—Thoreau providing the inspiration, Seeger singing on my stereo, Russell supplying the reading material—and whatever loneliness was involved was pretty much smothered by the intensity with which I filled up page after page of, yes, yellow foolscap, with my apprentice scribblings. By the time October ended, the cabin's small space heater was barely adequate against the chill, and by November, trying to draw my time out as far as possible, I could only write by putting the card table right up against the vents—my first lesson in staying warm while writing, but not my last.

I took hikes when I wasn't writing, fished for bass in the lake, or took frigid swims. The other thing I was doing, of course, was burning bridges, dropping out in flames so intense there was no chance I could ever rebuild a conventional career, making retreat impossible.

It was early in October when a notice caught my eye in the local paper. The old-time movie star Fredric March had a vacation home in town, and according to the article, his seventy-fifth birthday would be celebrated with a continuous, all-day showing of his films at a local prep school—a showing to which the public was invited.

March was of an earlier generation, but TV kept his reputation alive. *Les Miserables. Dr. Jekyll and Mr. Hyde. Death Takes a Holiday. Inherit the Wind. Seven Days in May. The Desperate Hours.* (This last was a favorite of mine, with Humphrey Bogart playing an escaped killer holding hostage March's family.) Whatever the role, March always projected an earnest sincerity that put him on a different level than most Hollywood actors, made him somehow "realer," the actor you would want as your father, or at least your uncle. There was a dignity about him that wasn't stuffy but seemed to come from a calm, modest sureness about who he was at his innermost core. He had manly intelligence, March did, and manly intelligence was something I was hoping to cultivate myself.

Politically, he was as liberal as anyone in Hollywood, and it was only his great stature that kept the yahoos of the Un-American Activities Committee off his back. I admired him for that, too.

My favorite March film was William Wyler's classic, *The Best Years of Our Lives*, which had won him an Oscar as best actor in 1947. I had only seen a truncated version on TV, badly mutilated by commercials, but even so, the power of the film had gripped me immediately.

Now, running down the schedule in the newspaper, I saw that this was the film scheduled to run last in the all-day screening, and after writing all morning I could easily make the short drive down through the hills.

The school was old New England, but its theater was state-of-the-art, and I had no trouble finding a seat near the front. I expected a big crowd, a film festival atmosphere, but what I found could hardly have been more different. At first, I was the only one sitting there, and then gradually a few more started drifting in—they were dressed a bit nicer than casual, suggesting guests who were attending a party, not a film. One of them, a boy of about twelve, bounced a tennis ball against the stage, and when it rolled over to me and I handed it back, he asked, pleasantly enough, "How long have you known Fred?"

Fred, I gathered, was going to attend in person. Instead of a crowded tribute, what I had stumbled into was a celebration thrown by March's colleagues and friends—open to the public, yes, but on a beautiful autumn afternoon I was pretty much all there was of the public.

The boy, my new friend, was the one who saw them first. He dropped his ball and ran over to shake March's hand the moment he came through the door. I didn't recognize him immediately; young people are not particularly good at making allowances for age, and, feeling like a party crasher, I was too shy to stare. Holding his arm was a woman I assumed must be his wife, Mildred Eldridge, the famous Broadway actress—together, without any fuss, they took their seats four rows directly behind me. With them was an attractive woman in her fifties, a white-haired man who had the weathered, seen-everything look of a retired deli owner, and, taking the last seat, a portly, pleasant-looking fortyish fellow with hooks instead of hands.

Once they were settled, one of the men sitting in my row climbed up onstage to say a few words of greeting. Since everyone knew "Fred," he didn't have to make introductions, but I understood from the context of what he was saying that the attractive woman was Teresa Wright, *Best Years* costar, that the white-haired man beside her was William Wyler, the film's director, and the smiling fellow waving one of his hooks in friendly acknowledgment was Howard Russell, the handicapped vet who had won a special Oscar for portraying "Homer Parrish," the film's young sailor who is trying to adapt to a handless life.

I hardly had time to peek at them before the lights went down and the opening credits rolled down the screen. A remarkable situation—it was like sitting in an easy chair reading *The Great Gatsby* with F. Scott Fitzgerald looking over your shoulder—but before I could give it the thought it deserved, I became caught up in the movie, swept along by its art.

It's the autumn of 1945, victory autumn. In the waiting room of an army air base, two recently discharged vets wait for a ride home to "Boone City" in the Midwest—and then the sergeant calls out their names: "Parrish! Derry!" Grabbing their duffel bags, they hop aboard a bomber to fly across the country, joined there by an infantry sergeant named Al Stephenson, who, momentarily taken aback by Parrish's hooks, laughs and gives them a warm, full-hearted shake.

They take up a position in the bomb bay, watch as the sun sets on the vast countryside below them. Parrish, after telling them about his fiancée waiting for him at home, falls asleep. "That Wilma sounds like a swell girl," Derry says. Stephenson takes a long, thoughtful drag on his cigarette. "Wil-ma," he says, exaggerating the syllables. "I hope for Homer's sake she's swell."

The only time I had seen the movie was on TV, so I wasn't prepared for its power. *Best Years* is still my favorite Hollywood film, as it is for many people my age. The cast was unbeatable. March as Al Stephenson, the banker-turned-sergeant-turned-banker-again, brings real humanity to the role and fully deserved his Oscar. Myrna Loy as his wife Milly is a perfect match, warm and companionably ironic. Dana Andrews gives the performance of his life as Fred Derry, the handsome air force bombardier brought, literally, down to earth. Teresa Wright as Peggy Stephenson does the girl-next-door better than anyone, playing her not just as an All-American good sport, but a real woman with real intelligence, and—she slowly builds this—real passion.

Harold Russell, the handless vet Wyler discovered at a navy hospital and coached into the role, steals every scene in which he appears, and there is never any doubting that his suffering and courage are real. Virginia Mayo as Derry's spoiled playgirl wife is much more than that; she makes us understand where her famous lament comes from when her marriage breaks up: "I gave you the best years of my life!" Hoagy Carmichael, of all people, appears as a piano-playing saloon keeper—his teaching Parrish to play "Chopsticks" with his hooks is a scene that's unforgettable. And let's not forget character actor Roman Bohnen, Derry's father, who, finding a crumpled paper left in Derry's haversack, smoothes it open and reads it out loud—a citation for his son's bravery in leading his squadron to the target while badly wounded. He finishes, wipes a tear from his eyes, takes a long puff on his cigarette—and manages to say more with that one puff than any smoker in any film ever made.

The story achieves greatness working on two levels at once. One is the perfect way it mirrors a very specific moment in America's history—the uneasiness felt when the war ended, this massive effort that, with victory, would surely lead to a brighter world . . . or would it? The other level, the one that brings greatness, is how in doing this it manages to dramatize situations and themes that continue to be universal. What separation does to love. The horrors of war. The necessity of courage and hope. It could all have been too pious, preachy, and obvious, but it balances just above these dangers, and works its magic by focusing on characters whose concerns, fears, and dreams still seem heartbreakingly relevant.

Memorable scene follows memorable scene. Homer crashes his hooks through a garage window so the neighborhood children who have come to peek at them can get a better look. Derry sits bolt upright in bed, caught by a nightmare, screaming out the names of his friends parachuting from a burning B-17. Al delivers a drunken speech at a welcome-home banquet put on for him by the bank, wherein he rips apart the whole capitalist system and then builds it back again upon his belief in the common man. Hoagy Carmichael tells Homer to relax and not worry about the future, since (he's playing an ironic little piano tune to underline this) the world will soon blow itself up. Peggy embraces Derry at Homer's wedding—one of the top five all-time romantic Hollywood kisses, which is saying a great deal.

There's a secret to the film's remarkable staying power, at least while boomers are still around. To anyone born in the years 1945 to 1950, watching *Best Years* is like watching the loving impulse that gave us birth. This is our parents' story, as they fought back from the dislocation of war, and, as a vote of confidence in the future, gave birth to our generation. I was born in 1948, and have always been curious to get a glimpse at the world I was born into; *Best Years*, for a lot of us, provides that prenatal peek.

This is what the film did for me on its own. Take this, then multiply the power by an order of ten, and you can begin to sense what I experienced watching the film in a small theater with the stars and director sitting four rows behind me. *Behind me* . . . That was the extraordinary thing within an extraordinary situation—the geography of it all. Our entire film-going experience is predicated upon those actors and stars being up there on the screen in front of us, and to have them sitting behind me, to be between them and their representations on the screen, seemed like an upside-down flip of the normal world.

William Wyler. Teresa Wright. Harold Russell. Fredric March. What could they have been feeling, watching their masterpiece after thirty long years? Amazement at how quickly the years had flown by? Pride in having accomplished such work? Vexation, that here and there they could have done better? An overwhelming bittersweetness? An odd feeling of remoteness, as if their characters existed now totally independent of their portrayals? Or were they, like me, totally haunted by the magic they had managed to create?

The movie finished with Homer's wedding, the lights came back on, but no one moved, not for a few seconds. There was applause, but it wasn't overwhelming, like at a gala or tribute, but quieter, more heartfelt, the handclaps of old friends. March gave a friendly wave, then became an old man again, the way he shuffled back down the aisle, reaching around to help along his wife. "Are you going on to Fred's house?" my young friend asked me near the door. I've regretted for forty years not saying yes.

(Still another memorable scene: The cab brings Derry, Stephenson, and Homer into town from the air base at the movie's start. Homer, when the cab pulls up before his parents' house, trembles from nervousness. "I know," he says. "Let's go downtown to Butch's place for a drink before we go home." March as Stephenson looks him right in the eye, says with infinite empathy, "You're home now, kid.")

This all happened in 1972. March died three years later. I wonder if he ever watched the film again.

JOSEPH CONRAD

Of all the harmless little human niceties that have become extinct this century, I regret one in particular: the habit men had of carrying photos of their loved ones in their wallets. "Here's the missus," a friendly salesman might say, sitting next to you on the plane when you were somewhere over Iowa, with three hours yet to go before arrival. "And this is my Tommy at the lake, and that one is the bass I was telling you about—isn't he a beaut?"

I only ever carried one picture in my wallet, pressed between cellophane where it stayed for nine or ten years before disintegrating—a photo of Joseph Conrad. I carried him there for inspiration, but more than once, having patiently admired someone else's photos, I was tempted to bring him out.

"This one is my hero, Józef Teodor Konrad Nalecz Korzeniowski, who you probably know as Joseph Conrad. Pole who wrote English novels, but only after imagining them in French and translating to himself as he wrote. Sea captain, survived all kinds of adventures, Hemingway being a wimp in comparison. Maybe you read his 'Secret Sharer' in high school? Or how about *Heart of Darkness,* the novella *Apocalypse Now* is based on? Here, just look at him; he was old when this was taken, but have you ever seen a face projecting such strength of character? Looks like he's squinting into a storm, no?"

Tempting, but I never inflicted Conrad on anyone, though there were plenty of times, needing some literary courage, when I opened my wallet and took him out. I loved Conrad because, more than anyone I was reading then, he was the writer who wrote for the art of it, for literature, bringing to the task great aesthetic fervor and no apologies. What's more, he wasn't the delicate hothouse aesthete you might expect from this, but the very opposite. Of all the men who ever wrote novels, Conrad was undoubtedly one of the toughest—in the nineteenth-century British merchant service, weaklings simply didn't rise like he had from ordinary seaman to the command of great ships. He lived his adventures before writing them down, and then, once he did write them down, went out of his way to tell us that writing was the hardest, most dangerous adventure he had ever been involved with—and this is a message my twenty-five-year-old self badly needed to hear.

Sailing a tall ship around Cape Horn in a blizzard is a brave and diffi-cult thing, Conrad told us. Writing "Heart of Darkness" is a hundred times harder.

How I found Conrad is a lucky story, but with some depressing overtones, since it illustrates so plainly the decline in serious reading between his era and ours. It's a story that involves my great-aunt Addie, my great-aunt Lydia, and my great-uncle Joe. None of them ever married, but kept house with each other for all their adult lives. Uncle Joe worked in New York in an early version of public relations, Lyd worked downtown as a secretary, while Addie stayed home and did the cooking. They were affluent, but not rich—the kind of middle-class people who, in that era, could afford to hire a servant, at least on special occasions.

When they died, I inherited their books, since no one else in the family was interested. Many of these were beautiful, leather-bound editions of the popular and important British novelists of their day. Judging by the bookplate on the flyleaves, they ordered these every Christmas from W. H. SMITH & SON BOOKSELLERS & STATIONERS 19-21 CORPORATION STREET, BIRMINGHAM, and had them shipped across the ocean to their home in New Jersey. Some of these were best-sellers by Horace Walpole, John Galsworthy, and J. B. Priestley, but they also had Hardy's later novels, and six or seven by Conrad, including a thirteenth (!) edition of *The Secret Agent*, a book that is now only read by English majors.

That's the sweet and bitter part: how beautiful these books are as physical objects, evidence of a time when the book was still cherished. How wistful to think that "ordinary people"—a woman who had never graduated high school, a man with two years of college, a secretary—would think it perfectly natural and fitting to buy these books and read them . . . read Hardy, Conrad, and even Chekhov!

Conrad has never been an easy read (though he's easier than late Henry James, a writer I never particularly admired). His style is complex and demanding, sometimes Mandarin, with self-reflexive sentences that can be overwhelming in their color, passion, and intelli-gence. Reading him first in these contemporary editions helped me enter his world on his own terms—the carefully sewn binding, the beautiful leather, the slight mustiness which seemed, as I began reading, the smell of significance—these all drew me in.

I worked my way through his earliest novels first: *Almayer's Folly* (which he wrote in his cabin on board his last command) and *An Outcast of the Islands*, revved up the quality several notches with *The Nigger of the Narcissus, Lord Jim,* and *Nostromo* (a first edition of which I found in a used bookstore selling for fifty cents), then came to the two masterpieces everyone agrees on, "Heart of Darkness," and *The Secret Agent.*

This last, written in 1907, reads like it was written a week ago, so contemporary is it in mood and theme. We've heard of film noire, but this is the novel noire, fiction at its very darkest—a story about a group of London anarchists who plan to blow up the Greenwich Observatory.

Mr. Vladimir, a Russian diplomat, explains to the double agent Verloc (whose day job is running a porno shop in Soho) his philosophy of terrorism:

> "A bomb outrage to have any influence on public opinion must go beyond the intention of vengeance or terrorism. It must be purely destructive. It must be that, beyond the faintest suspicion of any other object. What is one to say to an act of destructive ferocity so absurd as to be incomprehensible, almost unthinkable, in fact, mad? Yes, the blowing up of the first meridian is bound to raise a howl of execration."
>
> "A difficult business," Mr. Verloc mumbled, feeling this was the only safe thing to say."

Conrad's great theme is loneliness, unbearable loneliness, and whether a man or woman can withstand its moral and psychological weight. In his story "Amy Foster," a Slav peasant, on his way to America, is the sole survivor of a shipwreck, and is washed ashore on the English coast. Everyone in the village mistreats him, except Amy Foster, a quiet, homely girl who brings him food when he's starving and finally marries him. But she, too, when he becomes ill and starts raving in his native language, is seized with fear of his strangeness, snatches up their child, and abandons him to die alone—a story that surely had deep personal echoes for Conrad, living as he did, a Pole, an artist, in the very heart of philistine England.

One of my favorite novels was and still is *Victory*. It's a plot only Conrad could handle. A thoughtful, skeptical Swede named Axel Heyst, in exile from the world, ends up guarding an abandoned coal mine on a remote South Pacific island, assisted only by a Chinese coolie named Wang. Heyst rescues a girl named Lena, a bewildered refugee from "Zangiacomo's Ladies Orchestra," and then, as the two lonely outcasts finally let themselves fall in love, tragedy, which the reader has felt lurking offshore like some dark, evil Malay dhow, finally closes in. There are no nastier bad guys in literature than the trio that come after Heyst: the elegant, women-hating Mr. Jones; the amoral Ricardo Martin, Jones's "secretary;" the savage alligator hunter "Pedro."

Victory hit me hard, perhaps because I was going through something similar just then, at least emotionally. I felt like an exile, felt it would take a miracle to deliver me a love of my own, and, if it did, I would have to fight to keep her.

Here is Heyst at twenty, the son of a cynically intellectual father, preparing himself to face a world he already feared:

> The young man learned to reflect, which is a destructive process, a reckoning of the cost. It's not the clear-sighted who lead the world. Great achievements are accomplished in a blessed, warm mental fog, which the pitiless cold blasts of his father's analysis had blown away from the son.
>
> "I'll drift," Heyst said to himself deliberately. "This shall be my defense against life."

I learned a lot from Conrad, mostly through osmosis, though the explicit lessons in his famous "Prefaces" helped, too. He took chances in his fiction, brave chances, and I wanted to follow him on this; if writing serious fiction is an adventure, why not make it a risky one? He was a realist, but he pushed the realism hard with his imagination, which was the secret of his hold on me. When it came to describing place, he was unequaled; the ocean, of course, but he was good on cities, too—the London of *The Secret Agent* is more creepily convincing than anything in Conan Doyle. As a novelist, he cast his net wide, found empathy for a complex range of characters, subjects, and themes, and, this being my own instinct, it was good to have him, via his example, pat me on the back in approval.

As for what kind of man Conrad was in person, it's hard to pin him down. He was a Polish aristocrat, a sea captain, a genius, and that is not a mix the world has seen much of. He seemed stiff and aloof to many of his contemporaries, very much the master pacing the upper deck of his brig, and yet there's a playful side in his letters that makes you expect that much of this was a defensive professional veneer.

Conrad is due for a major revival. His time, quite literally, has come around again, the modern world being what it is. Terrorism. Piracy. The clash of cultures. For decades his subjects seemed to recede safely into the past, into quaintness, but here they are on our TV screens every night, and anyone who wants to understand the psychology of our era could do worse than go back and read his novels written a century ago.

You can't discuss Conrad without mentioning Orwell's famous backhanded compliment: "One of the surest signs of his genius is that women dislike his books."

Ouch. But then I've never met a single woman who admires him.

Tom Paxton

Winter by winter the cabins I rented moved me steadily north—north toward a vocation, north toward a life. Literally north, too, though it was just a baby step now, up to the northwest corner of Connecticut and the surprisingly wild and forgotten Taconic hills. I saw an ad in the paper by a woman who was offering reduced rent to someone willing to care for her plants. I answered it, and ended up with the nicest house I'd rented yet, set on an abandoned farm road called Cream Lane. A grand piano in the living room, a huge stone fireplace, a spiral staircase leading upstairs—and yet it wasn't elegant so much as cozy, shipshape, snug. This was the house people fantasized about when they dreamed of writing alone in the woods, and maybe the fantasy helped, along with the bright south-facing windows with their icicles clear as glass, because my stories finally took on some clarity themselves, made me feel I was making progress.

The staircase, the fireplace, the huge bed upstairs, all figured in fantasies of their own that winter, but solitude is solitude, and except for a weekly trip down to the high school to play pickup basketball, I spent that winter in monkish seclusion.

My landlady's husband was an interesting man—a documentary filmmaker who had spent World War II making movies for the Coast Guard (there was a picture of him on the wall shaking hands with Harry S. Truman), and now produced programs on classical music for public television. He had a huge record collection, the best stereo system I'd ever listened to, so it became a winter of nonstop music; I discovered Bartok through his records, deepened my love of Bach. He owned some oddities, too, for instance a big collection of sea chanteys, and nearly every album by someone I already admired greatly, Tom Paxton.

People who love music often come to associate certain years with the singers they were listening to just then, and for me that crucial winter of 1978, when I went from writing baby stuff to writing almost the real thing, has always been associated with Tom Paxton. I just have to play one of his albums and it all comes back. The way I would shove my writing desk from room to room following the sun. The funny/scary way the spiral staircase swayed under me when, tired from a long day's work, I corkscrewed up to bed. Those long afternoon walks across the open plateau behind the house. The snow that fell that winter in record amounts. How much care and attention I lavished on my landlady's plants. A good, a very good winter for me—and Paxton helped.

Of the folksinger-songwriters who came of age those years, Paxton seems to me the greatest talent. There was nothing fancy about him, nothing glitzy or egotistical; his whole demeanor was subordinated to his music and words. His voice was baritone, rising gently toward tenor when he sang one of his love songs, then sinking down toward bass when he turned angry and biting; in every song, the timbre seemed the one sincerity would choose if sincerity chose to sing. He looked like the no-frills Oklahoma "Ramblin' Boy" he really was, everybody's best friend—the kind of guy who almost begs you to take him for granted, which, of course, is often talent's best, most useful disguise. He went bald early, donned the Greek fisherman's cap he still wears today, and no sign of vanity or self-regard has ever crept further than that.

What set his music apart from Dylan's, Lightfoot's, or Phil Ochs's is a characteristic sweetness—not a saccharine sweetness, but a friendly, companionable kind that comes from surpassing gentleness and empathy. His love songs are among his best—"Leaving London," "Wish I Had a Troubadour," "The Last Thing on my Mind." *Didn't mean to be unkind* is a lyric from the last, and it's impossible to think of Dylan ever admitting that, just as it's impossible to imagine Dylan ever politely thanking the audience at the end of every song as does Paxton.

He is often compared to Pete Seeger, but he's more a commentator than Seeger, more a journalist responding to the foibles and tragedies of the day. He has a keen satiric sense, revived the "talking blues" to great ironic effect, wrote wonderfully funny songs for children ("The Marvelous Toy"), and, withal, could be as angry and bitter as anyone. No one wrote better antiwar songs about Vietnam, including "Talking Vietnam Potluck Blues," "Lyndon Johnson Told the Nation," and "Born on the Fourth of July."

Vietnam was the making of him as a songwriter, a writer of protest. Unlike a lot of people, he was just as angry twenty years later as he was at the time. Compare the satiric, biting mood of "Lyndon Johnson Told the Nation" ("Though it isn't really war, we're sending 70,000 more, to help save Vietnam from Vietnamese") to the raw, unflinching anger of "Born on the Fourth of July" ("I was born on the Fourth of July, no one more loyal than I, when my country said so I was ready to go, and I wish I'd been left there to die").

He never gave up writing topical songs, unlike Dylan who turned to rock, or Phil Ochs who tried turning to rock, then, perhaps sensing it was suicide to his talent, committed suicide. Paxton turned out to be the great sixties survivor, the songwriter who stayed ever-faithful to who he was, the true successor to Woody Guthrie—and it was Paxton who eventually wrote Ochs's epitaph, in a tremendously moving song called "Phil" ("I opened the paper, there was your picture, gone gone gone by your own hand; I know I'm going to spend the rest of my life wondering why, you found yourself so badly hurt you had to die").

The same grieving impulse made him write one of his finest songs, "No Time to Say Goodbye." It's a lament for everyone who ever suddenly lost a loved one, a song that is unbearably painful to listen to, but carries its own solace—and that's the kind of balancing act only the best songwriters have the wisdom and maturity to pull off.

HENRY BESTON

If you're going to do the writing-alone-in-a-cabin thing, there are lots of writers out there for inspiration—more than just Thoreau. Gavin Maxwell wrote several memorable books about living on the wild Hebrides coast of Scotland; John J. Rowlands has a minor classic called *Cache Lake Country*, about life in the Great North Woods; and even Richard Byrd—Admiral Byrd!—wrote a still very readable account of his winter alone in an Antarctic hut, *Alone*.

(Saul Bellow, who I semi-admired, supplies a corrective take on this, having the title character in *Ravelstein* opine: "All educated people make the same mistake—they think that nature and solitude are good for them. Nature and solitude are poison.")

The best of the cabin books, after *Walden*, is almost certainly *The Outermost House* by Henry Beston, first published in 1928 and never out of print since. Most readers have never heard of Beston, but there are a surprising number who include him in their top-ten list, and I rank him very high myself—no American writer, on any subject, ever had a better prose style than Henry Beston at his best. In 1927, with the deliberate intention of writing a book whose prose would match the beauty of the landscape he lived in, he built a hut facing the ocean on the great east-facing beach of Cape Cod:

> My house stood by itself atop a dune, a little less than halfway south of Eastham bar. I called it the Fo'castle. It consisted of two rooms, a bedroom and a kitchen-living room, and its dimensions overall were but twenty by sixteen . . . My house complete and tried and not found wanting by a first Cape Cod year, I went there to spend a fortnight in September. The fortnight ending, I lingered on, and as the year lengthened into autumn, the beauty and mystery of this earth and outer sea so possessed me that I could not go.

Beston talks about his "field naturalist's inclinations," but when it came to literary focus he was less a nature writer than a landscape writer, a seascape writer, a celebrant of the look and feel of the wondrous, ever-changing frame that encircles and enhances life. All his qualities are there in *The Outermost House*'s magic first paragraph:

> East and ahead of the coast of North America, some thirty miles and more from the inner shores of Massachusetts, there stands in the open Atlantic the last fragment of an ancient and vanished land. For twenty miles this last and outer earth faces the ever hostile ocean in the form of a great eroded cliff of earth and clay, the undulations and levels of whose rim now stands a hundred, now a hundred and fifty feet above the tides. Worn by the breakers and the rains, disintegrated by the wind, it still stands bold. Many earths compose it, and many gravels and sands stratified and intermingled. It has many colors: old ivory here, peat here, and here old ivory darkened and enriched with rust. At twilight, its rim lifted to the splendour in the west, the face of the wall becomes a substance of shadow and dark descending to the eternal unquiet of the sea; at dawn the sun rising out of ocean gilds it with a level silence of light which thins and rises and vanishes into day.

Lyric, of course, but the prose is ballasted by precision, so it never becomes purple—not for nothing does he spell out that his beach is *thirty miles* from the inner shore of Massachusetts, that it runs for *twenty miles* north and south, that its rim stands *a hundred, a hundred and fifty feet* above the tides. He describes the cliff's colors without using a "normal" color word: *old ivory, peat, old ivory darkened and enriched with rust.* And here, too, is Beston's signature rhythm which he maintains throughout the book—a rhythm, a beat, an impetus which is lulling and powerful at the same time, like ocean tides. Read Beston out loud, especially the final paragraph of ever chapter, and you'll catch the rhythm yourself—and note how it's enhanced by his characteristic trick of suddenly switching, for a few lines, to the present tense.

All of Beston's books are worth reading, and I've managed to collect most of them over the years, including his hard-to-find *A Volunteer Poilu* about his experiences driving an ambulance in World War I, two volumes of fairy tales written for children, and a very precious first edition of *The Outermost House*. His *Northern Farm* about his life on a Maine pond just inland from the coast is still a favorite of mine, and *Herbs and the Earth* is nearly as good. One morning, browsing through a used book store near his farm, I found a book that once held a spot in his library, *The Voyagers, Being Legends and Histories of Atlantic Discovery* by Padraic Column; Beston's name is handwritten on the endpaper, *Henry Beston*, in that beautifully elegant old-time script that no one has the patience now to bother learning.

Beston, because he was so attuned to the earth's ancient verities ("elemental" was his favorite word), had remarkable prescience. What he feared was a mankind so divorced from nature that all kinds of ugly cultural aberrations would result, corroding our souls. He wasn't alone in this; if you read American nature writers starting with Thoreau in the 1840s and running all the way through Rachel Carson, Edward Abbey, and Wendell Berry, you realize that they saw into the future better than any economist, scientist, or pundit, few of whom were smart enough to envision our environmental doom. Beston sensed where we were heading as a civilization as early as 1946, when he concluded *Northern Farm* with these prophetic words:

> The chromium millennium ahead of us is going to be an age whose ideal is a fantastically unnatural human passivity. We are to spend our lives in cushioned easy chairs growing indolent and heavy while intricate slave mechanisms do practically everything for us as we loll. What a really appalling future! . . . What has come over our age is an alienation from Nature unexampled in human history. It has cost us our sense of reality and all but cost us our humanity. We have become vagabonds in space, desperate for the meaninglessness which has closed about us.

Beston never doubted that in *The Outermost House* he had written a classic, and just before he died he received confirmation of this when the Fo'castle was designated a "National Literary Monument," and a plaque erected on its weathered shingles reading:

THE OUTERMOST HOUSE IN WHICH HENRY BESTON, AUTHOR-NATU-
RALIST, WROTE HIS CLASSIC BOOK BY THAT NAME WHEREIN HE SOUGHT
THE GREAT TRUTH AND FOUND IT IN THE NATURE OF MAN.

Beston's wife, writer Elizabeth Coatsworth, describes how the seventy-eight-year-old Beston (still handsome, he resembled the old Frederic March) was just strong enough to attend the ceremony on the dunes:

On each side lay the everlasting sea, bright in the sunshine and whipped to whitecaps by the October wind. There were four or five speeches, and Henry gave a few words in response to the crowd which so warmly and lovingly faced him. The little house had been twice moved, once because a gale had washed away the sand to its very steps, a second time because the wind had hollowed out the dune beneath the building so it was about to collapse. Now in its third position it nestles like a partridge close to the marsh.

To Henry, this was as it should be. Dunes might come and go, and so might men and women, but now he felt that his work had achieved its destined place, and he was satisfied.

Snug in my own Fo'castle (albeit one with a grand piano), I would have liked to face elemental forces myself, a la Beston. Elemental forces were not normally what the Connecticut woods dished out, but what they did offer—intimacy, quiet, a surprisingly forgotten kind of wildness—did me good. The winter settled in early, with the first snow before Thanksgiving, and most mornings when I looked out the window from my desk, the sun, reflecting off the snowpack, shone up as much as down. This clarity, the brightness, burned itself into my thinking—never had my imagination felt sharper, never had I felt so close to my characters and ideas.

After Christmas a warm spell set in; the snow melted far enough to reveal old cornstalks in the fields, but then it turned cold again, and the sky took on the damp pewter look that presages something (at last!) elemental.

The weather report that morning confirmed this—it talked about heavy snow. I drove my Volkswagen down to the village to stock up on supplies, drove back again, meaning to unload the groceries and get everything arranged, but fell asleep on the couch first. The truth was I wasn't feeling particularly well, and I figured a nap would help me snap out of it.

When I woke up after dark I was shivering—or was I sweating? My clothes were so damp it was hard to tell. I looked out the window, saw it snowing furiously, in white glutinous flakes that seemed to veer sideways and stick together as they fell. I switched on the lamp, but nothing happened. The electricity was out—this was getting interesting—and with the electricity out, the furnace wouldn't work, which explained my shivering. Or partially explained—for it was apparent now that I was sick, truly sick, sick as in the flu, aches and pains, fever and vomiting. There was just enough acuity left within my mental fog that I could make a cold-blooded inventory of what I faced. A blizzard, a big one. The flu, a bad case. Electricity, kaput. Heat, nonexistent. Food? Locked in my VW, buried in the snow.

I built a fire in the fireplace, managed to build a crescent of warmth into which I squeezed most of my landlady's plants, giving them a chance for survival. That left me to worry about, though I was largely past that stage by then. The house shook in the wind, literally shook. One shake snapped the electricity back on—the flash of it startled me awake on the couch—but it only lasted a second and went out again, leaving me colder than before. I think it was about that time, my fever peaking, when I became convinced there was someone beating on the door with their fists.

The night seemed as long as ten normal nights, thirty normal nights. I may have slept a little toward dawn. If anything, it was snowing even harder now, with icy pellets that tattooed the window glass and sluiced down the chimney. My fever may have abated some, and, weak as I was, I began to get the germ of a grimly audacious intention. There was no reasonable way to get through the day ahead without being crushed by loneliness and despair. None. But so what? I could sit down and bloody well do what I always did in the morning—I could write.

And this is how I spent the remainder of the famous Blizzard of '78—writing a short story on a manual typewriter, freezing my butt off, stopping to make frequent trips to the toilet to puke, swaying on the chair from weakness, shaking from fever, but somehow cranking out those words. I was one kind of writer when I woke up that morning, a sick, cold, feverish wannabe, and I was a different kind of writer when I finished those brutal four hours at the desk—a sick, cold, feverish semi-real-thing.

A few days later, reading the Boston newspapers, I was saddened to learn that Henry Beston's Fo'castle had been a casualty of the blizzard. Its dune had collapsed in the flood tide and it had been swept out to sea—sad, but when you think about it, the very fate the Outermost House deserved.

Man at Her Best

BEVERLY SILLS

I fell in love with Beverly Sills two or three years before everyone else did. This was the New York City Opera Sills, before celebrity struck, not the Metropolitan Opera Sills, the one who after her famous debut there had her face on the cover of *Time*, started appearing on all the talk shows, became the friendly, marketable "Bubbles" even opera haters adored.

My Sills was the local girl who made good, the child singer who had worked her butt off, done all the grunt jobs a company soprano gets called upon to do, singing roles her voice had no business touching, but all the while perfecting her technique, until she got her big chance in City Opera's 1966 production of Handel's *Julius Caesar* and became a star seemingly overnight. An *opera* star, not a crossover celebrity—the distinction is important. Now she could pick and choose what roles she performed, but her loyalty was still to City Opera; this is where I saw her sing, where the magic of her coloratura and the sensitivity of her acting captured me while she was, at least in mega-celebrity terms, still flying beneath mass culture's radar.

It's an interesting point about admiration, this business of discovering someone before the rest of the world catches on. It can make you possessive and jealous, turn you into the kind of bore that goes around saying, "I saw her in her prime well before all this fuss," but it can also give you a proprietary interest in someone's career, a stake in their acceptance by the world at large. BEVERLY SILLS IS A GOOD HIGH! read the button on sale in the State Theater's lobby, and I wore mine with pride, even when she started appearing on Johnny Carson and many of her old fans wrinkled their noses in disgust.

That she became "Bubbles," the charming, self-deprecatory, semi-dumbed-down good sport all America fell for, is something I could forgive her for, since celebrity seems as good a disguise as any to hide your talent under; as ever, I was drawn to artists who used their personalities as camouflage. Sills had come up the hard way, went about the star business with uncommon modesty and good sense, and had a voice so beautifully melting it could make a grown man cry. Can *still* make a grown man cry, as I discovered last night when I played her last-act aria from *Traviata*. Whatever coloring she put into her voice, whatever shadings, intimacies, and passion, it went straight to my heart.

My love for opera had continued growing since those teenage days when I'd accidentally stumbled upon it on the radio in my darkened bedroom. By the time I was twenty, I'd accumulated a modest collection of vinyl albums, those boxed sets that were produced so lavishly they were like miniature opera houses you could pay twelve dollars for and tote proudly home beneath your arm.

I loved opera's richness of sound, the ardent, old-fashioned spirit that animated it, even—especially!—the melodramatic and improbable plots. As a bona fide late-twentieth-century ironist, I was starved for extravagance and spectacle, and opera supplied these big-time, opening a window in my spirit that for too long had been shut. My especial love became duets, trios, quartets, quintets, sextets; opera is the only art (well, okay—ballet, too) where upwards of six characters' varying emotion can be expressed simultaneously, and I never tired of how Mozart, Verdi, or Puccini managed to interweave these multiple emotions and sounds.

Inevitably, my listening led me to Sills. WNYC in New York had a Sunday-morning opera program, and on one of these I heard her recording of the final aria from Douglas Moore's *The Ballad of Baby Doe*. As operas go, this is a realistic one, based on true events—the rise and fall of Colorado silver baron Horace Tabor, and his love for his young bride, "Baby Doe." The final scene shows Baby Doe after Tabor's death, returning to the last mine he owned, the "Matchless," living alone in a cabin into great old age. Her final aria, "Never shall the mourning dove," sung as the snow falls, combines the forthright optimism and strength of an old-fashioned Methodist hymn with the wistful yearning of a lullaby, in a combination that is as heartbreaking as anything in opera. Sills sung this perfectly, and while I had missed her name when the opera began, I made sure I was ready with pencil and paper when the recording ended and the announcer gave the cast.

When you fall in love with something from a distance, it can often be difficult to make that first crucial step toward requiting that love—hard not to be just an armchair traveler but to actually buy the plane ticket; hard to get up the nerve to ask the cute brunette out for coffee; hard, in my case, not just to listen to opera at home but actually go into Manhattan and see one. There's an odd inertia you have to overcome, part laziness, part shyness, that tends to make you want to continue worshipping safely from afar. You sometimes need help in taking that first step, the magnet drawing you must be strong, and in my case, with opera, it was Sills who powered the attraction, Sills who drew me out of my shyness and got me off my butt.

This was in one of her most famous roles, Mary Queen of Scots in *Maria Stuarda,* Donizetti's bel canto showpiece. City Opera had mounted a new production for her, which was going to be followed by two other "queen" roles, *Anna Bolena* and *Roberto Devereux.*

New York City Opera in the '70s was at the height of its reputation, and many opera fans thought that this is where the real operatic action was, not at the Met. Its home, the State Theater, was built with George Balanchine's New York City Ballet in mind, and there was always someone grumbling about its acoustics, but to me, walking up the stairway that first time, it could have been La Scala. The seats those years were ridiculously cheap; $3.50 got you a seat in the balcony, and $5.50 brought you down to a three-row-deep mezzanine with unobstructed views of the stage. These became my favorite seats; there were many Saturdays when, down on one of my visits from Connecticut, I would buy a ticket for the matinee, watch it, go and wander the West Side for a few hours, buy myself a crepe for dinner, then come back for the evening performance and still have change left from a twenty-dollar bill.

On that first time, my wedding night to opera, I felt bashful, very much the opera virgin—Would it hurt? Would I respond appropriately?—but all this disappeared once the lights went down.

There, right below me, beautifully dressed lords and ladies of the English court gathered to meet Queen Elizabeth, and, looking directly up at me, began to sing.

Qui si attende, qui si attende, De'Bretanni la Regina—and there is no exaggerating the effect this live sound had on me; compared to recordings it was like sky compared to photos of sky, ocean compared to postcards. My ears felt the aural equivalent of shortness of breath—they inhaled deeply, expanded, breathed in a deep, exhilarating way that years of listening to vinyl had never managed to achieve.

Thirty seconds into the performance I was in real love with opera, consummated love, not puppy love from afar. Maria Stuarda doesn't come onstage until the second act, and when Sills finally appeared, the audience erupted into an ovation that affected my ears much like the music did, lifting them onto an entirely new level of admiration. This is the girlish, wrongly accused Mary Stuart, and Sills was dressed accordingly, in a simple maidenly cloak. She was the prisoner of her cousin Queen Elizabeth, but now she sang an aria of innocent delight in her temporary freedom. *Guarda; su'prati appare, odorosetta e bella, la familglia de'fiori.* ("Look; in these fields appear fragrant and fair flowers of every kind, and on me they are smiling.") As her aria deepened, Sills stooped to pick them like a girl.

And, even though she was in her mid-forties then, there was still something girlish in Sills's face, or rather, she seemed balanced on the border between girlish and matronly, which isn't a bad place for a soprano to teeter, given the variety of roles she's called upon to play. I always saw a lot of New York in her looks, though what exactly I was reading is hard to say, other than that you saw faces like hers on secretaries riding the subway to work.

The one thing most people know about opera is that the soprano is always fat. Sills wasn't fat, but attractively full-bodied; a dandy of the 1890s, had she lived then, might have lecherously twirled his mustache and opined that she was "a fine figure of a woman." Size in opera singers isn't a bad thing, anyway, as it helps with those chest tones, and helps even more in making them larger-than-life figures to inhabit opera's larger-than-life world. Sills was comfortable with her body; that was the important thing. Her movements were graceful and surprisingly lithe, and came from a deep physical intelligence that matched the intelligence so obvious in her eyes.

As for her voice, it had that same girlish-matronly blend. Singing high, it could be playful, almost frivolous, trilling those ornamental cadenzas like someone juggling ice cubes made of champagne, but when it deepened you could sense the mature, sexual woman behind it, and it was this combination that made her special. There was a great deal of vulnerability in her voice, and it always seemed engaged in a gentle pleading, trying to make the audience understand where her character's emotion came from. It wasn't an immaculate column of sound her voice created; it was more like a reaching, yearning hand.

Sills was an extraordinary actress; even if she had never opened her mouth she would have made *Maria Stuarda*'s old-fashioned melodrama totally believable. As the opera ends, Mary is led from the Tower of London to the courtyard where she will be beheaded. The City Opera production milked this for all it was worth, with the block dominating the stage, and behind it a leather-hooded executioner waiting with a sharpened ax. Sills's costume was the same modest cloak she had worn earlier, but now, as she finished her final aria (*Anna, addio; Roberto, addio! Eil mil sangue innocente versato plachi l'ira del cielo sdegnato*), she took off the robe and underneath was revealed a stunningly beautiful red gown, the red of the Stuarts, an unrepentant Catholic red to match Sills's flaming red hair, which, the executioner advancing, she knelt and arranged over the block to await the inevitable as the curtain fell.

What drama! What tragedy! What fun! The audience went wild— never at a play, never at a sports event, had I heard such applause and cheering. Sills came on last to take her curtain call, and it was revealing how she did so. No grandstanding sweep of the hand and arm, no deep curtsey, no clutching her hand oh-so-humbly over her heart. Sills walked on briskly, waved to us, then nodded, nodded quickly up and down, nodded like someone facing old friends, not an audience. It was a modest gesture, instinctive, just right—and because it was so natural, so obviously like her, it went right to our hearts in a way a more-theatrical gesture couldn't.

(I heard Sills interviewed once about modesty's limits. On her first appearance at La Scala, wanting to be a good sport during rehearsals, she noticed that no one was paying her any attention. The next day, picking her moment, she tore her costume at the sleeve, screamed in Italian about how shoddy it was, threw a tantrum worthy of the bitchiest diva who ever lived—and from that moment on, La Scala took her *very* seriously indeed.)

Sills was always a hard ticket, but I managed to see her sing five more times before she retired. *La Fille du Régiment* showcased her great gifts for comedy. In *Lucia di Lammermoor*, the tenor was a young José Carreras; one of the complaints you heard about City Opera was that they had no tenors good enough to match Sills, but in this performance, they did.

One lucky night, having bought a ticket for *Traviata* starring a soprano I'd never heard of, a spotlight came on before the overture and the company's director, Julius Rudel, came out onstage to say that the soprano was indisposed, and they had managed to secure a last-minute replacement: Beverly Sills. The audience erupted. Violetta was one of her greatest roles, but she hadn't sung it in years, and, as Rudel explained, she was going to perform with no rehearsals whatsoever. You wouldn't have known this, of course. Sills inhabited the role with such naturalness that the stage business hardly mattered, and, in any case, she knew instinctively just when and where to move. The next morning's *New York Times* had a front page story about this, it being such an irresistible twist on the usual understudy-makes-good theme.

I saw her triumph under equally difficult conditions during *I Puritani*. Rudel came onstage to say the tenor was ill, but that they had arranged for a replacement to fly down from Montreal. He was awful, croaked his way through the first act of Bellini's notoriously difficult music, and then Rudel came on before the second act to say that this tenor too was indisposed, and that a student understudy had gallantly consented to take his place. The night of three tenors—but it hardly mattered, we only cared about Sills, and despite all the stress she sang as deliciously as ever.

The last time I saw Sills sing was as the three heroines in Offenbach's *The Tales of Hoffmann*—opening night of a new production—and it still stands in my memory as the most exciting opera performance I ever witnessed. That this was only partly due to Sills needs some explaining. She was wonderful, of course. As the mechanical windup doll Olympia, she was not only hilarious, but touching; as Giulietta, the Venetian courtesan, she was seductive and sensuous; as Antonia, the consumptive ingénue, she sang herself to death (as the plot requires) so convincingly you could glance along the aisle and see people sob.

A triumph, but it wasn't only Sills's, since for perhaps the first time in her career she was thoroughly upstaged. *Hoffmann*'s three villains were played by Norman Treigle, the company's basso, who had always flirted with fame, but never quite achieved it. He had sung *Julius Caesar* the night of Sills's great triumph in 1966, sung the father to Sills's *Louise* in a famous production, and had become a City Opera legend as the devil in Boito's *Mephistopheles*. He was thin, cadaverous, even scary; his voice was as deep and rich as Pinza's, but it was his acting people talked about the most. He inhabited his roles with such conviction and intensity that it put him on an entirely different level than even good actor/singers could manage; as one critic put it, "Treigle believed to the point of fanaticism in opera as total theater."

Treigle never sang at the Met, but he was gradually establishing an international career in Europe. He was the singer opera lovers talked about when they talked about underrated talents, and City Opera fans were as proud and possessive of him as they were of Sills.

The three bass roles in *Hoffmann* are "devil" roles, and opera never had a more convincing devil than Norman Treigle. Watching him perform, you wouldn't have been surprised to learn that he had sold his soul to the devil at an earlier point in his life; or perhaps he really *was* the devil, and had struck a deal with God that allowed him time off to play himself in opera. Now, on opening night of this important new production, it was simply impossible to take your eyes off him, he was so oily and malevolent, evil and unctuous, slithering around the stage like a poisonous eel. *Hoffmann* ends with a postlude in a tavern, but this production, in a risky bit of stage business, eliminated that, and ended with Treigle as the violin-playing "Doctor Miracle," springing up on a platform in the audience to sing in triumphant, orgiastic glee as Antonia slumps lifeless to the stage.

Take the loudest ovation I ever heard Sills earn, double it, and you can get an idea of the sound that greeted Treigle when he came out for his curtain call. Years later, when Sills came to write her autobiography, she lingered on that moment, describing how bewildered she felt during the performance, seeing Treigle, this trusted colleague she had worked with so often, totally ignore the stage movements they had carefully rehearsed, literally upstaging her, going off on his own, dominating the performance with his improvisations and his voice. As angry as she was, she understood and even sympathized with what was going on—that this was Treigle's desperate attempt to earn the celebrity that was his due. "If Norman wanted it so badly," Sills wrote, "I could only go along."

Treigle had his triumph, but couldn't enjoy it very long. He died a short time later, alone in a New Orleans hotel room, of a perforated ulcer.

When Sills retired, she devoted her considerable energy to playing a role that came natural to her: the diva as regular guy. She partnered Carol Burnett in comedy specials, sat in for Johnny Carson on *The Tonight Show*, hosted a talk show of her own; as one writer put it, "She can be credited with an almost one-woman popularization of opera in this country through her intelligence, frankness, humor (and terrifically infectious guffaw), and enthusiastic willingness to proselytize without showing any operatic mannerisms."

The writer got that right—no one ever had a more contagious laugh than "Bubbles" Sills. She knew sadness in her own life—one child was permanently institutionalized with birth defects, and the other, Muffy, was born deaf and never heard her mother's voice—but her intelligence and tough New York genes triumphed over everything. She assumed the directorship of City Opera, made it the first prominent opera company to use the super titles they all use now, and later in life, after chairing all sorts of good causes, became a commentator on the Met's radio broadcasts.

That was the last time I ever heard her voice, and her intelligence and laugh were as lively as ever. She died a few months later, in July 2007. Learning of this, I immediately went downstairs for my old vinyl *Baby Doe*, put the last record on the turntable, placed the needle down on the last groove, listened as Sills sang again those stirring words in that heartbreakingly beautiful voice that one day, hopefully long in the future, I'll gladly listen to in lieu of last rites:

Never shall the mourning dove
weep for us in accents wild.
I shall walk beside my love
who is husband, father, child.
As our earthly eyes grow dim
still the old songs will be sung.
I shall change along with him
so that both are ever young
ever young.

MARIA CHEKHOVA

To find Chekhova, I first had to find Chekhov.

This was another happy result of inheriting my aunts' and uncle's books. I'd broken both elbows in a climbing accident out in British Columbia (climbing up, then falling over a campground fence on my way to climbing school), and, with lots of free time on my hands, I decided to tackle Chekhov. *The Works of Chekhov*, a collection of his stories and plays, was bound in a cheap version of what used to be known as "Moroccan" leather, and soft red bits of hide dribbled down on my chest as I read—and dribble still, as I discovered just now when I went to my bookshelf to take it down.

It was published in 1929—a thick and varied compilation, with enough Chekhov masterpieces that I fell in love with him three stories in. "The Kiss." "In the Ravine." "The Black Monk." Never had I read stories that inhabited the form so wonderfully, caught the poignancy of life so perfectly; they came with that remarkable lucidity and truth that descended upon a handful of Russian fiction writers in the nineteenth century in a way those qualities never descended on any similar grouping before or since. And while many apprentice writers take Chekhov to be all about smallness of plot and modesty of theme (what at a later evil date became known as "minimalism"), I took away from him just the opposite lesson. I was amazed at how wide his reach was, at least when it came to the variety of human types he included in his work. Peasants, princes, doctors, writers, soldiers, actresses, shepherds—even woodcock, dogs, and cats. Chekhov could inhabit all of them, and write from the fullness of his empathies.

I found a photo of Chekhov, and since I already carried Conrad in my wallet, hung him up on my wall. Toward the end of the book were his plays, and *The Sea-Gull* became another brick in the base of the artistic credo I was trying, with my heroes, to construct. I'd seen it performed in London starring Joan Plowright, Laurence Olivier's wife, as the vain and imperious Madame Arkadina. I'd also seen a wonderful version on PBS starring Kevin McCarthy (an underrated actor I much admired; the only fame he ever achieved was for his role in the cult film, *Invasion of the Body Snatchers*), and the beautiful ingénue, Blythe Danner.

Now, actually reading the play on the page, reading it a second time, reading it a third, I began to understand that Chekhov includes in the play his finest statement about what it is to be a writer. But he plays a trick with this. Instead of putting his credo in the mouth of Trigorin, the famous established writer, or Constantine, the talented/tormented beginner, he gives the lines to Nina, the aspiring actress, when she returns to the villa near the lake after a disastrous attempted at establishing a career.

She takes Constantine's hand, recalls their youthful, innocent love, then tells him this:

> So you've become a writer. You're a writer and I'm an actress. We're both caught up in the vortex . . . When I act, I rejoice, I delight in it; I am intoxicated and feel that I am splendid . . . Since I got here I have been walking all the time and thinking, thinking and feeling how my inner strength grows day by day. And now I see at last, Constantine, that in our sort of work, whether we are actors or writers, the chief thing is not fame or glory, not what I dreamed of, but the gift of patience. One must bear one's cross and have faith. My faith makes me suffer less, and when I think of my vocation I am no longer afraid of life.

The gift of patience. When I think of my vocation I am no longer afraid of life. The words seared themselves into me, or why else did I read them over and over? Now, looking back from the perspective of forty years, trying not to blush over what is surely the only possible word to end this sentence with, I realize the place they seared themselves into was my soul.

Whenever I fell for a writer's writing, I went and read their biographies; I knew no other writers, even after I had published my first two books, so this was the only interaction with mentors or colleagues I had. Learning about Chekhov's life, my admiration for him only increased (reading bios of other writers—Hemingway for instance—my admiration sometimes went down). His personal story was compelling: the son of peasants, forcing the "slave" out of his soul by a tremendous act of will, becoming a doctor, dashing out those humorous early sketches, then suddenly discovering that his talent was far greater, that it demanded of him far more. Women often fell in love with him, especially after the success of his plays, but he didn't marry until late (to the young actress, Olga Knipper), and by then he was already suffering from the tuberculosis that would kill him at the height of his powers, age forty-four.

Reading about Chekhov, you learn how close he was to his remarkable family, especially his younger sister, Maria. She never married, but devoted herself to supporting her brother's work, acting now as his secretary, now as his nurse and housekeeper, now as his literary agent, and always as his closest confidant and friend. "It was not just that Maria adored her brother," biographer Roland Hingley points out. "She was also an educated woman who could appreciate his subtler writings and enter his more complex preoccupations."

One fact hit me hard about Maria Chekhova—she outlived her brother by fifty years. What did she do with herself, after collaborating so closely with a genius? What filled her life when her beloved brother was no more?

I stumbled upon the answer inside a footnote in a compilation of his letters called *Anton Chekhov's Life and Thought,* edited by Simon Karlinsky. When Chekhov could no longer hide from himself the implications of his TB, he sat down and wrote a letter to Maria that surely ranks as one of the simplest, most eloquently moving wills in history:

Dear Maria,

I bequeath to you my house in Yalta for as long as you live, my money and the income from my dramatic works. You may sell the house if you so desire. After you and Mother die, all that remains is to be put at the disposal of the Taganrog municipal administration for the purpose of aiding public education. I have promised one hundred rubles to the peasants of Melikhovo to help pay for the highway . . . Help the poor. Take care of Mother. Live in peace among yourselves.

Anton Chekhov

Yalta, August 3, 1901

Karlinsky footnotes this letter thus:

Far from selling the house, Maria made it into a Chekhov Museum, and devoted the remainder of her long life to maintaining it. With single-minded devotion, she defended it from looters during the civil war that followed the October Revolution, saved it from nationalization by getting it assigned to the Lenin Library in Moscow in the mid-1920s, rebuilt it after it was damaged by an earthquake in 1927, and stayed in it during the German occupation of the Crimea in 1941.

This wasn't all. To curry favor with whichever authorities were currently in power, Maria was willing to wildly distort her brother's themes and friendships, so, under Lenin, she filled the library with Lenin's books, in order to make visitors think he was Chekhov's favorite writer; under the Nazis, she hung a portrait of Gerhart Hauptmann to emphasize her brother's links with German literature. "She saw as her task in life the preservation of her brother's house and the encouragement of future generations to read his writing. To achieve these basic objectives, she was prepared to make considerable concessions and adjustments."

This simple footnote got me thinking, not only about the poignancy of someone surviving a person they loved by fifty years, but also the unspeakably brutal history that this half-century represented, and exactly what "concessions and adjustments" Maria would have had to make in order to preserve her brother's work. I would leave the idea for a time, my imagination would busy itself elsewhere, but always returned that same nagging conviction: that Maria's story was so compelling it could only be told by a novel. Not just any novel, either, but the kind that might have been written by her brother himself, part short story, part dramatic play, so, in telling the story of Maria's devotion, it would pay homage to Chekhov, too.

The result, some five years after the idea first came to me, was *Chekhov's Sister.* I did more research, collected every quote about her I could find from Chekhov's biographers and friends, then realized, now that I had a firm sense of the woman, that I had to create my own Maria separate from this; only when the imagined, fictional Maria became more real than the real "Maria" could I begin at last to write.

She is first described in the "play" format, as she prepares to face the Germans entering Yalta in 1941:

Maria Pavlovna enters from the right, carrying beneath her arm two pictures in ornate gold frames. She is a youthful woman in her seventies, taller than average, with traces of auburn in her otherwise gray hair. Her forehead is wrinkled, but tightly; her cheeks are as smooth as a young girl's. Childless, a spinster, there is about her a strength and directness that suggests great fecundity; her hips and breasts are full, for instance, and the only sign of her solitude is the yearning, absent-minded way she strokes herself, even in company. Her eyes are brown flecked with blue and remarkably coquettish; her smile ironic, as if she knows full well how ludicrous the effect is. In this irony, in the curious tilt of her head and the dark eyebrows (thick and brooding by the bridge of the nose; thin and merry by the edges), she resembles her brother, Anton Pavlovich Chekhov.

In life, Maria formed only one other serious attachment besides her brother—a pleasant, rather commonplace man named Alexander Smagin, who her brother talked her out of marrying—not by saying anything explicit, but by his total silence whenever she mentioned his name. In the novel, many years later on a trip to Moscow, Maria has a chance meeting with Smagin who she hasn't seen since she refused him:

"I am alone in the world," Smagin tells her. "I am alone in the world, Maria Pavlovna, as you yourself are alone. And yet you are not yet forty and there is still time. You are still a young woman, Maria. We made our mistake, but there is still time to correct it."

He was sobbing so much his face became splotchy, then distorted and grotesque. She turned away from it in horror and began walking slowly up the street.

"There is still time, Maria Pavlovna!"

It was as if all her bitterness was rising up to mock her, springing back after she had throttled it for so long, and she covered her ears and kept on, longing for him to follow and stop her and yet walking even faster for that reason.

"Maria Pavlovna, there is still time!"

She tried summoning up her brother's face to gain courage, but the image wouldn't come, and instead she saw the faces of all his characters, the poor, the saddened, the solitary, and then she realized she wasn't imagining them at all but making right toward there in the middle of the pavement, the dense throng of the heartbroken, their collars turned up against the cold, and just when she decided she must swerve to get around them, Smagin's voice faded away into silence, the crowd parted, and she was accepted into the space Antosha had left for her there all along.

A year after the novel came out, I received a letter from a woman named Katia Jacobs in New York:

One reason your novel touched a responsive chord is that Anton Chekhov and his sister were close friends of my family. Specifically, my grandfather Isaak Altschuller, a tuberculosis specialist, was Chekhov's doctor in Yalta; my father remembers sleeping on the couch in Anton's study to keep from catching his siblings' measles. Both my grandfather and Maria Pavlovna disapproved of Chekhov's young bride, Olga Knipper—I think they thought that Anton's many journeys to see her and the plays in cold distant Moscow hastened his death. My grandfather's friendship with Maria Pavlovna continued after he emigrated to Germany.

I went and looked up Altschuller's name in the biographies—and yes, there he was, referred to in the next-to-last letter a dying Chekhov ever wrote Maria, where, after complaining about the useless medicine he was taking to ease his pain, writes, "I recall with gratitude only the heroin Altschuller once prescribed for me."

Ms. Jacobs's letter gave me much to think about; there was the real Maria Pavlovna who I took and turned into *my* character, and now here she was, "real again," giving me the uncanny feeling she had stepped out from the novel's pages into life.

Maria, it's good to know, made up with Olga Knipper as both women grew older; Olga's annual visits to Yalta were much anticipated occasions that for both women became the highlight of their year. There is a remarkable photo taken at the very last of these reunions in 1957. The two women sit next to each other on a bench outside the villa/museum in Yalta—Olga, very much the famous actress in retirement, still beautiful through all the wrinkles, still proud, and next to her Maria's shriveled, feisty visage is all but blotted out by an enormous pair of black glasses, the kind a 1950s advertising man may have worn on Madison Avenue.

If you find this photo, stare down at it closely, for what you are looking at is one of the twentieth century's greatest survivors—a woman who ran the gauntlet of the most horrible history imaginable, and yet came through not just with her own skin intact, but carrying with her the precious gift of her brother's art.

Winslow Homer

There is something about the natural history of admiration that makes it difficult to love all the arts equally. Opera fanatics will flock to a performance of Britten's *Billy Budd,* but never pick up Melville's original novella; poetry lovers can know all about Lowell, Sexton, and Plath, and next to zero about Bach, Bartok, or Berg; ballet freaks may never once in their lives have been to a serious play. Though many flirt and some sleep around, art lovers tend to be monogamous, and they sign on to their passion for life.

Which is to say: There are embarrassing gaps in my love of the arts. Drama would seem to have been a natural fit for me, but there were no local theaters where I grew up, Broadway was too expensive even then, and I was getting so much melodrama from opera, there wasn't room for anything tamer. The only playwright I was crazy about was Chekhov, and even with Chekhov it came mostly from reading the plays, not live performances.

Visual art is an even sadder story, since it's not easy to explain why it never captured me the way literature and music did. But, come to think of it, maybe it is easy. I had no aptitude for drawing or design, so emulation was entirely out of the question; if I had no talent for music-making either, at least with music you can tap your heels, wave your arms about, hum along with it, dance. Color was something I responded to passionately, but outdoor color, untamed color, the palette of clouds, sun off water, the chiaroscuro of sunset and sunrise. (That bringing this beauty indoors was exactly art's point I was slow to pick up on.) Impressionists, when I saw them, seemed too smugly bourgeois; abstract seemed phony; the great religious paintings I shied away from like a vampire. Clearly, there was a philistine blank spot in my soul that the visual arts couldn't reach.

Exceptions existed, artists whose work I stumbled into and liked just enough to make me regret not admiring them deeper. Henri Rousseau, for instance—for years, a copy of his *Jungle Sunset* accompanied me on my moves. (Lush flowers, pliant ferns, and there, nearly hidden toward the bottom, a tiger sinking its fangs into a native's throat; why that once spoke to me so powerfully I'd just as soon not know.) The New York Ashcan School I admired, too, etchings and prints by John Sloan and his disciples ("apostles of ugliness" critics called them, dismayed by their gritty realism). N. C. Wyeth I'd loved since I was a boy; Rockwell Kent's epic rebelliousness appealed to me, too—but then it wasn't surprising, loving books as I did, that the art I was most familiar with was illustration.

The great exception to my ignorance was Winslow Homer. I knew his early *Harper's Weekly* prints from my Civil War buff days, and his New England connections made me think of him as the visual equivalent of Robert Frost. When I learned that he painted fly-fishing subjects, my interest was really piqued; all it needed was a lucky break to blossom. And then I read that the Whitney Museum, the "old" Whitney off Columbus Circle, was mounting the largest-ever retrospective of his work. I went, I saw, I stared—and by the time I descended back onto 59th Street, my eyes glazed with Homer's seeing, I was hooked for life.

I love Homer for the reasons everyone loves him. His accessibility and depth. The nostalgia; the glimpses he gives us of innocent, trusting, exuberant childhood, and, with it, the reminders of what this country was like when it too was young. What he does with the ocean, how his seascapes elicit from us feelings that, without ever crystallizing, seem to hover over something wondrously profound. "Meditation and water are wedded forever," Melville told us, and it's this marriage we see in Homer's work.

There are reasons that his art spoke to me more personally, studying his work at the Whitney on that first visit. His paintings are realistic, but suffused with imagination, which is the blend I was trying to achieve in my own work. He loved New England's characteristic look and feel—the high upland meadows tossing with uncut hay; the one-room schoolhouse with its weathered red sides; the craggy headlands with moonlight illuminating the surf—and as I moved deeper into New England, discovered forgotten pockets little changed form Homer's day, I began to appreciate the landscape through his eyes—learned, thanks to Homer, where the color was on drab days and where the shadows were on days that were blindingly bright.

Most of all I loved his fly-fishing paintings, those old-timers in canoes on Adirondack ponds, or the lonely figures tossing streamers toward the roaring Saguenay rapids in Quebec. Here I had an avocation I pursued passionately, and here Homer was the one undoubted genius that avocation had created, at least in America. If you went fishing, could choose any writer, photographer, or painter in history to bring along to record what beauty and insight you caught, it could only be Winslow Homer.

Reading about the man, you realized he took his work very seriously, but never displayed the slightest trace of ego or narcissism; he lived a simple, working life on the coast at Prouts Neck in Maine, and a simple working life in the country is how I wanted to do things myself. (And not *over*do; "Winslow Homer was notoriously difficult to approach, guarding his privacy and hoarding his words like some social skinflint.") His biographer describes him as "a small, dour-looking man with a bushy Civil War–style mustache; he looked for all the world like a successful and somewhat rakish stockbroker." As for his lifestyle: "[T]he life that I have chosen," he once wrote his brother, "gives me my full hours of employment for the balance of my life. The sun will not rise or set without my notice and thanks."

Everyone knows his most famous paintings, and it takes seeing the originals to snap you out of the dangerous overfamiliarity that can dull admiration up. In *Eight Bells*, the seamen standing near the rail of their ship dressed in sou'westers and oilskins seem made of the same primitive, eternal stuff the sea is that frames them; in the calm, steady way they stare down at their sextant, the men seem a match for anything the elements can dish out. In *Summer Night*, two girls waltz with each other on the rocks by a moonlit sea, as a cluster of townspeople silently stare; beauty dancing in darkness pierced by light—there's Homer's imagination for you, there's the characteristic Homer touch.

Snap the Whip has those boys flinging each other across the meadow at recess, making us feel we're kids again, the last ones on line, until our heads spin with giddiness and it's hard not to fall down. In *The Dinner Horn*, our whole vanished rural past is captured in the graceful figure of the young woman calling her family in to lunch. *The Gulf Stream* gives us a dismasted boat surrounded by storm clouds, a water spout, and circling sharks—and, withal, the solitary black castaway reclines across the transom as if all this is as nothing compared to the unshakable serenity he tosses back at fate.

When Homer traveled to the Adirondacks or Canada, it was to relax, so it's not surprising that his fly-fishing watercolors are quieter, more intimate and reserved than his more-famous canvases—less involved with the broad implications of fate, and more concerned with beauty for beauty's sake. Anyone can appreciate them, they have that generous Homerian accessibility, but a fly fisher will recognize moments that only come to initiates, when you're searching the water with a fly rod, searching deeply, and becoming alive to impressions in a way that is far more receptive than if you sat by the water and merely stared.

He captures the curves of fly fishing, Homer does. The unscrolling arc of a line in a graceful backcast; the dimpled circles of trout rising on a lake; the gentle upward undulation of a trout's bright flank as it leaps; the dipping curves, bow and stern, of a canoe being portaged on a guide's shoulders. He captures fly fishing's colors, from the slate grays of a North Woods lake at dawn (*Two Men in a Canoe*) to the lush, Rousseau-like yellows and greens of bass fishing in Florida (*Homosassa Jungle*). Half of his fishing paintings seem to be of still lakes and tranquility, but half pose the fly fisher near waterfalls or rapids, and show the surprising drama that's the other part of the sport's appeal. In *Fishing the Rapids, Saguenay River*, he remembers his seascapes, poses the fly fisher as a small figure casting bravely from a rock on the very edge of the most tempestuous yellow-brown rapids imaginable; the lonely, over-dwarfed fisherman casts his line out with hope, determination, even defiance, so what is ostensibly an illustration of a fishing scene becomes a bold statement of faith in mankind.

Homer, never a man to brag, in writing to his beloved brother Charles once said this: "You will see, in the future, I will live by my watercolors." A century after his death, we know this was no understatement. I never look at Homer's work without feeling better about the world, or, in parallel, feeling so deeply its haunting mystery.

This last can best be seen in a work not too many people know, since reproductions never hang in summer camp bunkrooms or on investment bank walls. It's called *The Sleigh Ride*, and is one of the rare Homer watercolors set in winter. A horse-drawn sleigh is seen just before it disappears over the crest of a snow-covered hill. It is night out, dark, and the only light comes from a slight break in the clouds and the moon's icy reflection off the tracks left in the foreground by the sleigh's runners.

The horse pulling the sleigh is just barely visible, and seems created out of the same stuff as the purple-black lines of trees rising in the distance; the figures in the sleigh, only slightly more visible, partake of the elemental substance of the night clouds, and seem to be returning, not to a warm farmhouse, not to a cozy inn, but to the sky which created them. It's a painting that is extraordinarily chilling, and not just because of the snow—wherever these people have come from, wherever they are bound, we will not see them on earth again.

Chilling—and healing, too, so powerful is the sense of an inevitable fate there is no use struggling against. There on that snow-covered hill is a borderline we can only resign ourselves to and cross. The only consolation Homer allows us is the bright glint off those iced-over tracks—the brief, transitory flash of beauty our passage leaves in the crust of life.

JUSSI BJORLING

Life now took an operatic turn—operatic, at least if you focus on the happy first act, when the love-starved young tenor falls in love with the ethereal soprano, and they sing rapturously as they fall into each other's arms. Celeste was a recently graduated nursing student on her way to a job in Colorado. I was still living rented-cabin-to-rented-cabin, but with my first novel published, I felt I was at last making progress. It was difficult to conduct a long-distance romance between Colorado and Cape Cod, and after flights back and forth and too much money spent on phone calls, we decided the sensible thing was to live together, see if what we felt for each other was strong enough to consider marriage.

We moved to the hill country of western New Hampshire, near a teaching hospital (for her) and trout streams (for me), bringing with us our total worldly possessions, which included a colander, two typewriters, six fly rods, Celeste's Plymouth Duster, and our favorite vinyl record albums, which we tried, with varying degrees of success, to turn into the other's favorite.

My albums were top-heavy with opera. When people asked me what I missed about New York, I said what everyone says—"The delis!"—even though what I really missed was going to the State Theater or the Met. But, thanks to records, you can be an opera fanatic in the boonies, and as soon as Celeste left for work in the morning

I would stack my favorites up on the stereo and listen on and off throughout the day. This might be Lotte Lehmann, singing one of her famous Wagnerian roles, or it might be one of the great American sopranos like Rosa Ponselle or Leontyne Price. Tito Gobbi, the great Italian baritone, was a favorite, as were Maureen Forrester, Bidu Sayão, Leonard Warren, Feodor Chaliapin, and Kathleen Ferrier.

As much as I loved their voices, I loved the great tenors even more; there is something about that powerfully sweet, very difficult to produce sound that went straight to my heart. The tenors I admired made a long and varied list. Caruso, of course—the static you had to listen through somehow made his voice seem even more authentic and appealing, as if he were reaching out to you through the fuzzy scrim of time. Tito Schipa, whose career was made in Italy during the 1930s, singing lirico-spinto roles with a wistful, compelling sweetness. Lauritz Melchior, the great Danish heldentenor, whose ringing notes, singing *Lohengrin*, would make the windows rattle in their sashes. Fritz Wunderlich, the great interpreter of Mozart and operetta, who, according to the album notes, had died in his thirties falling down the stairs. The great contemporary tenors, too—the young Luciano Pavarotti, and even younger Placido Domingo (a crossover artist for us; his duet of *Perhaps Love* with John Denver became the song we danced to at our wedding). And then veterans no one knew outside the opera world, but who could sing with the best of them, Carlo Bergonzi and Josef Traxel.

Before leaving New York, I had managed to see a fair number of world-class tenors in person. Franco Corelli was a matinee idol at the Met, not only for his Latin-lover good looks, but for his wildly passionate voice. Richard Tucker I saw in *Simon Boccanegra* just before his untimely death; while he was the world's worst actor, he sang rings around the foreigners who made up the rest of the cast. The Canadian tenor Jon Vickers I heard several times; Peter Pears, Benjamin Britten's lifelong partner and collaborator, I saw in Britten's *Death in Venice* at the Met, a role created for him, and I still remember the ovation he received when, an old man now, exhausted, he walked slowly out from the wings for his curtain call.

I admired them all—listening, my vocal cords would tense in sympathy as they gathered in their breaths for the last high note—but the one I admired most was Jussi Bjorling.

Bjorling died in 1960, so I knew his voice only from records. He was born in Sweden in 1907 into a musical family; his father had studied at the Met, his mother was a concert pianist, and Jussi started singing professionally at the age of five, when he toured the U.S. with his father and brothers in the "Bjorling Male Voice Quartet." (Vintage recordings of them still exist; Jussi, not surprisingly, steals the show.) He made his debut with the Stockholm Opera in 1930, and began an international career five years later at the Vienna State Opera. Three years after that, he began singing at the Met, where he appeared frequently until his far-too-early death.

Apparently, he wasn't much of an actor, but in his era opera singers were expected to do most of their acting with their voice, and here he was unsurpassed. Critics loved him. "Jussi Bjorling possessed an absolutely faultless technique, superb evenness of tone and amazing breath control. The great natural beauty of his voice and the elegance and good taste of his singing, achieved without loss of passion or dramatic power, are always apparent" (Laurence Feldman). "There was a shine on his sound from the first, and he was musically exemplary in everything he did. He had a beautiful gift, and he used it not only well but wisely" (Irving Kolodin). "The haunting beauty of Jussi Bjorling's voice set the tenor apart from all others while he lived" (Howard Klein). "Whatever Bjorling's voice sings about—things grave, happy, tragic or reflective—it seems the last word to be said on the matter. The voice is beautiful beyond telling" (Edward Woodson).

A voice, particularly a tenor's voice, can be a hard thing to throw adjectives at. "Haunting" certainly describes Bjorling's voice, but it also begs the question—haunting *how?* His combination of sweetness and power does it for me, a wistful strength that sounds like a contradiction, but, in Bjorling, manages to coexist in a way that can be, yes, haunting. In almost everything he sang, in the most remote part of his voice, implicit in the tone but never actually heard, is the sound of a strong man crying—crying for love, crying in happiness, crying in heartbreak. This isn't the audible, Canio-like sob that Caruso interpolates in his arias, but something more poignant, since it seems to skip our ears and enter straight through our heart. A vulnerable voice, though it never faltered; a triumphant voice, though it never left its hurt entirely behind.

The producer of many of his recordings, Richard Mohr, sensed this, too.

"I always felt that regardless of the music, an opera aria or anything else Jussi ever sang, underneath it all there was always this tone of sadness. He could sing 'Funiculi, funicula,' and I could hear sadness in it. I don't know why, I just think it was a basic quality of the voice, less a matter of interpretation than an inherent quality in the vocal equipment."

In operatic terms, his was a lirico-spinto voice, which means his repertoire included much of Verdi, all of Puccini, and French add-ons like Massenet, Gounod, and Bizet. His recording of "Celeste Aida" in 1936 taught the Italians to sing it right; his "Salut! Demeure Chaste et Pure" always stopped the show when he sang *Faust;* his 1951 duet with Robert Merrill from *The Pearl Fishers,* "Au Fond du Temple Saint," is a best-seller even today. The recording he made with his fellow Swede, Birgit Nilsson, of *Turandot,* is considered to be one of the top-ten opera recordings of all time. (Characteristically, the Bjorling aria you remember from *Turandot* is the gentle "Non Piangere, Liu," not the showier "Nessum Dorma" that later became Pavarotti's signature.)

His voice darkened toward the end of his life, and he began singing roles like *Otello,* at least on records; he had an extraordinary way with art songs, too, and his recordings of Rachmaninoff's *In the Silence of the Night,* or Beethoven's *Adelaide* are as beautiful as anything he ever sang.

Bjorling did not look like what his voice might lead you to expect. He was short and stocky like a great many tenors; if you put an apron on him, a floppy hat, he would have resembled a baker. In person, he could be hard to deal with, and many descriptions tiptoe around his fondness for alcohol. "Bjorling could be difficult as only the extremely gifted can be. The mere physical effort of getting him onto stage or into town, or, for that matter, into your country, put managers through hell." The booze, the constant stress of travel, the extraordinarily high expectations he had to live up to night after night, all played a role in his early death.

Bjorling married a soprano, and there is a recording of them in *Cavalleria Rusticana,* but it lacks the fire of a later recording he did with the great Zinka Milanov. His son Rolf was a tenor, too, and I saw him sing once in New York; he wasn't bad—he could have made a career there—but everyone, when he opened his mouth, expected his father's voice to emerge, and so our admiration for Jussi poisoned our admiration for him.

I've never seen anyone comment on something that is perhaps too obvious to mention. Of all the animals, man, at his or her best, is capable of producing by far the most beautiful sounds. Listening to Sills, listening to Bjorling, we understand exactly how extraordinary this ability can be; it raises mankind in our estimation the way a great athlete or dancer exalts us by the miracle of what can be done with the human body. Despair for our race, what we've done to our planet? Listening to the great voices doesn't let us off the hook, but at least it throws another consideration into the balance, and if we had to appeal to the universe for forgiveness, we'd be smart to use Caruso's voice, or Pavarotti's, or Jussi Bjorling's.

PART THREE

Still Admirable After All These Years

HERMAN MELVILLE

As an attitude toward life, admiration ages better than most. Its worst threat, disillusionment, is most apt to strike in your twenties and thirties, and if your heroes can survive this, then they're safe to accompany you through the rest of your life. The people we admire become part of our texture; as we grow older, this texture thins a little here, thickens a bit there, but the part that comes from purest, deepest admiration, generating all those positive antioxidants, often remains flexible and strong.

There are dangers, of course. There are changes. Old admirations can be clung to so stubbornly they crowd out new ones—the arteries of admiration can harden just like real arteries. New admirations can make you neglect old ones—the process can sometimes work in reverse—but this is rarer, and in any case, new heroes tend to find us by climbing on the shoulders of those we worshipped when young. A son gets us to listen to a hip-hopper he's crazy about, and at first we're appalled, but then we remember Lionel Hampton bopping on the vibes, Ella Fitzgerald singing scat, Dylan Thomas reading his poetry, and yes, we get it now, that hip-hopper doesn't sound half-bad after all.

But if I'm brutally frank with myself, it's clear my golden age of admiration occurred in the years from age twelve to thirty-five, when my capacity (and need) to admire was absolutely at its peak. Once I married, started raising a family, the hours tightened up, there was less time to spend reading, listening, and watching, or, to put it another way, looking down at my infant son, looking down at my toddler daughter, I was lost in admiration almost all the time, though admiration of a very different sort than what I've tried in these pages to describe.

The natural history of admiration has its senescence just as it does its youth, and while the changes aren't bad ones, they're worth taking a few minutes to try and pin down.

Along with four million other high school kids my age, I was assigned to read *Moby-Dick*. Unlike three and a half million of them, I actually read it; unlike 499,979 of those who did, I immediately read it a second time; unlike all but a handful of the remainder, I've never stopped reading it since. It's impossible to exaggerate my admiration for Melville and his great book—but I'll take a crack at it. Smelt all the people I've celebrated here into a gold bar, place it on one side of a scale, place the gold bar of Melville on the opposite side, and the two sides would balance, or come damn near.

It can be a bit obvious and embarrassing, a writer worshipping Melville. Just last week at our town dump, sorting out the recyclables, I noticed a man, a friend, advancing on me with a video camera. Had I sorted things wrong? I wondered—was I about to get busted? No, nothing like that. My pal was producing a mini-documentary for our local library to promote reading, and he was going around the dump asking the more literary-looking dumpers what they thought was the great American novel.

"*Moby-Dick*," I said at once.

My friend's expression sagged; clearly, he was expecting something more original.

"Yep, *Moby-Dick*," I said again. I thought about it, though I didn't have to, then squinted the camera right in the eye. "Indisputably, *Moby-Dick*."

The whaling lore, the cetology? I loved it. The Shakespearean monologues issuing from the mouth of a Nantucket whaling captain? Sounded most natural to me. The symbolism, the allegory? They didn't throw me; I went right to a semi-radical interpretation, understood the novel to be a mystery to *feel*, not a puzzle to *solve*. For didn't Melville tell us right there in the first chapter what the pursuit of the white whale was all about? "It is the image of the ungraspable phantom of life, and this is the key to it all"—what could be plainer than that? If this *is* the key, then only those willing to accept that the novel's meaning is ultimately ungraspable (and haunting and tormenting for that reason) can truly respond to the novel's genius; those critical overinterpretations that have sprung up on Moby's back like so many bloodsucking remora are only that, overinterpretations, and undervalue the mystery at the book's core.

I admire not just the themes, but also the characters. There is Starbuck, the American everyman at his best, ready to courageously face anything in the world, except Ahab's monomania; "Starbuck was no crusader after peril; in him courage was not a sentiment, but a thing simply useful to him, and always at hand upon all mortally practical occasions." There is Stubb, the second mate, a "happy-go-lucky Cape Cod man," who, while he can't begin to understand Ahab's mad quest, ends up having a grudging respect for it; "Damn me, Ahab, but thou actest right; live in the game and die in it!" And let's not forget Bulkington, the man who steers the *Pequod*, and appears only twice in the book ("this six-inch chapter is his stoneless grave"), but then grandly. "Take heart, take heart, O Bulkington! Bear thee grimly, demigod! Up from the spray of thy ocean-perishing—straight up, leaps thy apotheosis!"

And of course Ishmael, the common man who quietly goes about his business but misses nothing—Ishmael, who has some of the same fatalistic, "desperado" humor as Stubb, and realizes early on (when he's dumped out of the whaleboat on the first lowering) just exactly what he's signed up for. "That odd wayward mood I am speaking of, comes over a man only in some time of extreme tribulation; it comes in the very midst of his earnestness, so that what just before might have seemed to him a thing most monstrous, now seems but part of the general joke . . . Now then, thought I, unconsciously rolling up the sleeves of my frock; here goes for a cool, collected dive at death and destruction, and the devil fetch the hindmost."

As with the Bible, you can judge a person's character by what passages in *Moby-Dick* appeal to them most. For me, it was always the passages that were the blackest, most fatalistic on one hand, and the most exhilarating and optimistic on the other:

Round the world! There is much in the sound to inspire proud feelings; but whereto does all that circumnavigation conduct? Only through numberless perils to the very point whence we started, where those that we left behind secure were all the time before us.

Were this world an endless plain, and by sailing eastward we could for ever reach new distances, and discover sights more sweet and strange than any Cyclades or Islands of King Solomon, then there was promise in that voyage. But in pursuit of those far mysteries we dream of, or in tormented chase of that daemon phantom that, some time or the other, swims before all human hearts; while chasing such over this round globe, they either lead us on in barren mazes or midway leave us whelmed.

That's for down. This is for up.

And there is a Catskill eagle in some souls that can alike dive down into the blackest gorges, and soar out of them again and become invisible in the sunny spaces. And even if he for ever flies within the gorges, that gorge is in the mountains; so that even in his lowest swoop the mountain eagle is still higher than the other birds upon the plain, even though they soar.

This was Melville talking about himself, or could have been, and it was something like the admiration I would feel for a soaring "Catskill" eagle that I brought to my worship of his work. At times, he was all but invisible in the heavens (*Moby-Dick, Benito Cereno, Billy Budd*), and other times he sank down into the gorges (*Pierre, The Confidence Man, Clarel*), but those gorges, his confused, despairing sloughs of despond, were a hell of a lot braver, bolder, and loftier than most other novelists' high points, and I became a Melvillian for life.

As for Melville the man, it took a long time for my admiration to simmer down to a level where he became fully believable. As a young man, I viewed him as people do Jesus and Lincoln—his halo made me blink. It was only after I'd been writing many years, been involved in struggles that on a minor level were similar to his, that I began to understand him as a person; only when my own career started facing heartbreak that on a minor level mirrored his, did I begin drawing upon his example for inspiration.

Melville's post-*Moby-Dick* career, the saddest story in American literature, has been told many times. How the reviewers either ignored his masterpiece or damned it; how his British publisher neglected to include the last chapter; how, with scarcely a week to rest and regain his energy after finishing *Moby-Dick,* he plunged into writing *Pierre,* the nearest thing to a nervous breakdown in print by a great writer we have; how Hawthorne, the one person in the country who could conceivably have understood him, turned his back on him completely; how his family began thinking he was insane; how he took a hack job on the Hudson River docks to make ends meet; how, when a British admirer came on a pilgrimage in the 1880s, no one in New York could say with certainty whether Melville was even still alive.

But let Lewis Mumford (a writer and thinker I greatly admire) pick up the story, in the prologue to the biography he wrote in 1929, which itself was one of the first important steps in Melville's resurrection:

When Herman Melville died in 1891, a literary journal of the day, *The Critic,* did not even known who he was . . . The older generation remembered that Herman Melville had once been famous. He had adventured into the South Seas on a whaler, he had lived among the cannibals; and in *Typee* and *Omoo* his fame had been founded. It was a pity, most thought, that he had not done more in this line, for his later books, obscure books, crowded books, books that could be called neither fiction nor poetry nor philosophy nor downright useful information, forfeited the interest of a public that liked to take its pleasures methodically. In *Moby-Dick,* Melville had become obscure; and this literary failure condemned him to personal obscurity . . . The writer about whom all these sage banalities were written, shares with Walt Whitman the distinction of being the greatest imaginative writer that America has produced.

From this sad story, it's possible for an American writer to draw semi-opposite conclusions. The first is the obvious one: that even if you write a masterpiece, it will be misunderstood or ignored, especially if you have no literary cronies to hyperbolize your worth ("All fame is patronage," Melville wrote. "Let me be infamous.") The second is that if you *do* write a book that is misunderstood or ignored, you should not give up writing—that you should in fact write all the harder the deeper the neglect is, even if your determination not to quit becomes half-demented.

This is how my admiration for Melville changed once I experienced a tinge of his disappointment and pain. Sometimes he seemed to be walking ahead of me on our snowy dirt road when I took my afternoon walks through the New Hampshire twilight—a lonely figure well muffled, but with an unconquerable something about his posture that I could suck my gut in, throw my shoulders back, and imitate myself.

Uncomprehending critics? Fuck 'em! Publishers breaking contracts or cheating on royalties? Rot in hell! Mediocrities ruling the day? Bring 'em on!

Melville, despite the world's indifference, with more and better reasons for quitting than possibly any creative artist ever faced, never stopped writing in the forty years that followed *Moby-Dick*, and left on his desk when he died a masterpiece, *Billy Budd*. All the sadness of his life becomes nothing when measured against this. He never gave up—and if Melville didn't give up, why should we lesser worms, with such smaller provocations, give up ourselves?

My career hit a bad spot after some early success, where it didn't just feel like indifference and neglect were my lot now, but actual punishment and abuse. I'm not the only writer who goes through spells like this, where self-pity threatens you from one side, bitterness from the other. I was just smart enough to understand that I'd better do something about it quick. I needed some major-league encouragement, and maybe Melville could provide some as he had before, though this time I wouldn't go to his books to find it, but to the place he actually lived. And so, on a cold April weekend, my wife and I found an overnight babysitter for the kids (something we'd never done before), got in the car, drove down along the Connecticut River, then turned west through the Berkshires into the pastoral Housatonic Valley where Melville once lived.

For all my admirations, I've never been one to go on pilgrimages. Constraints of money and time played a part, but the main reason is that I always carried my heroes *with* me, so I didn't need to travel to see them. Then, too, I worry that seeing where they lived and worked might somehow tarnish them—how well the modern world can tarnish!—and this is what has kept me away from Walden Pond, which I've taken long detours to deliberately avoid.

But our mini Melville pilgrimage turned out to be fun, and, yes, restorative. Our first shrine was Monument Mountain, a steep little peak (a "headless sphinx," Sonia Hawthorne called it) rising above the Housatonic in Stockbridge. Here on August 5, 1850, occurred the most famous short hike in American literary history, when a party that included Melville, Hawthorne, and Oliver Wendell Holmes, ascended through the mountain laurel to the summit for a happy picnic. This was the first time Melville and Hawthorne ever met; they were caught by a thunderstorm on top, and took shelter under the boulders. Once the rain left off, Melville "bestrode a peaked rock, which ran out like a bowsprit, and pulled and hauled imaginary ropes like a sailor."

(Nathaniel Hawthorne, whom I admire as a writer, always seemed lacking as a man. He never went out of his way to help Melville's career, he was condescending to Thoreau, and he was a Franklin Pierce, pro-slavery Democrat during the Civil War.)

After climbing Monument—it was cold; the wind snapped from the northwest; the views were expansive across three states—we drove to the Berkshire Athenaeum in Pittsfield to visit its "Herman Melville Memorial Room," with its priceless collection of mementos from his life and career. This is holy ground for Melville lovers; included are such rarities as the desk he wrote *Billy Budd* on, a pipe he bought on his honeymoon, family portraits, and, most poignant of all, a little official badge he wore as customs inspector on the New York docks during the long years of his literary eclipse.

"Look at this!" I called to Celeste, as I moved along the display cases. "Oh my god! And this!"

In 1850, having already begun *Moby-Dick*, the head of a young family that included not only his wife and baby son, but his mother and sisters, tired of Manhattan with its incestuous literary life and bustle, Melville decided to buy an old farmhouse and 160 acres of farmland on the outskirts of the market town of Pittsfield—he called the farm "Arrowhead" for the Indian souvenirs he found while tilling. After the confusion of moving in, he soon established a routine he was to follow during his eleven years here, as described in an early letter to Hawthorne:

> Do you want to know how I pass my time?—I rise at eight—thereabouts—and go to my barn—and say good-morning to the horse and give him his breakfast (it goes to my heart to give him a cold one, but it can't be helped), then pay a visit to my cow—cut up a pumpkin or two for her and stand by to see her eat it—for it's a pleasant sight to see a cow move her jaws—she does this so mildly and with such a sanctity. My own breakfast over, I go to my work room and light my fire—then spread my ms. on the table—take one business squint at it, and fall to with a will.

Happy times, but the current of Melville's life never ran smooth for long. In 1852, Melville decided to dedicate *Pierre*, his seventh novel (the nervous breakdown novel) to the mountain that dominated the view from his study window—and it's a brave and poignant thing to dedicate a novel to a mountain, suggesting that, after the incomprehension that met *Moby-Dick*, there was not a soul in the world he could turn to for solace. The dedication reads:

> To Greylock's most Excellent Majesty. In old times authors were proud of the privilege of dedicating their works to Majesty. A right noble custom, which we of the Berkshires must revive . . . since the majestic mountain, Greylock, my own most immediate sovereign lord and king—hath now, for innumerable ages, been one grand dedicatee of the earliest rays of all the Berkshire mornings, I know not how this Imperial Purple majesty . . . will receive the dedication of my own poor solitary ray.

Celeste and I toured the house, noted how cramped the old farmhouse must have been with so many people living here, how cold it would have been in winter—though dominating the downstairs is the massive black chimney that is the central "character" in the story, "I and My Chimney." ("Some say that I have become sort of a mossy old misanthrope, when all the time I am simply standing guard over my mossy old chimney.") Preserved with the house, the reconstructed piazza (immortalized in *The Piazza Tales*) overlooks the cornfield Melville once so laboriously plowed. We walked across it, admired the view of Greylock, found a small white stone I put in my pocket to take home to New Hampshire (you'd be surprised the number of times I pick up that rock each day), then went back inside to see the room we had saved for last: Melville's upstairs study, with a small brass plaque reading IN THIS ROOM HERMAN MELVILLE WROTE MOBY-DICK OR THE WHALE 1850–51.

There is much in Melville's life that was unutterably tragic and dark; it's easy to focus too much on the evil enchantment that seems to have taken hold of him after the publication of *Moby-Dick*. Visiting his home, stooping slightly to peer out his study window, it's good to remember that other Melville, the writer at the height of his power, the vivacious friend who, everyone agreed, could tell stories better than anyone, the athlete who could still lead the others scampering across the hilltop rocks.

Here in his Arrowhead study he was at his peak, with the Berkshire winter coming on and he back at work at his desk. The world that is building in him is miraculously reflected by the world he can see outside; Greylock out his window matches the whale inside his head, so when he reaches for his simile it's right there before him: "and in the wild conceits that swayed me to my purpose, two and two there floated into my inmost soul, endless processions of the whale, and, midmost of them all, one grand hooded phantom, like a snow hill in the air."

PARKER PILLSBURY

The times can be so discouraging they force you to turn for solace to the past—Melville wasn't the only nineteenth-century hero I was clinging to for inspiration. The Reagan and first Bush years I remember as truly awful, at least if you paid attention to what passed for civil life. Bullies were in the ascendant, zealots, angry backlashers, not only in Washington, but in state government and even on our local school

who provided his state's resistance to the Fugitive Slave Law with its catchy slogan: "No slave hunt in our borders / no pirates on our strand / No fetters in the Bay State! / No slaves upon our land!"; Thomas Wentworth Higginson, the crusading minister who backed up his faith with deeds, leading a black regiment in the Civil War (and surviving to one day "discover" Emily Dickinson); Wendell Phillips, the wealthy Brahmin "turncoat" who became the movement's most eloquent orator; William Lloyd Garrison, publisher of *The Liberator*, facing down the mobs trying to lynch him, throwing their anger back in their faces with words just as hot.

"I am in earnest—I will not equivocate—I will not excuse—I will not retreat a single inch—AND I WILL BE HEARD!"

The abolitionist I developed a special interest in is not as famous as the others: Parker Pillsbury. I came upon his name first in Thoreau's journals, then, reading more, discovered that he was someone who both Thoreau and Emerson admired greatly. He wasn't an affluent Bostonian like many abolitionists, but a New Hampshire farm boy who had clawed his way to an education, become temporarily a minister, then used his religious faith to mount vitriolic attacks on the church's acceptance of slavery; with his friend Stephen Foster, he led the "come-outers" who invaded New England churches during Sunday service and demanded that their congregations, if they truly believed what they professed, get up and leave:

> Working as a wagoner, Pillsbury had earned tuition to put himself through Andover Theological Seminary (whose leader, Moses Stuart, constantly preached the God-given right of white Americans to own slaves), but gave up the ministry when forced to choose between abolition and the church. He had a leonine voice, described by James Russell Lowell as "tearing up words like trees by the roots." . . . He prized his patches and shredded coat, manhandled by many Sunday congregations . . . The come-outers were flamboyant, even reckless, but their purpose was to startle the conscience of the slumbering parishes, to rivet attention on clerical responsibility in a moral crisis. Pillsbury was not indulging in exag-

geration when he concluded, "Nothing like it so stirred the whole people until John Brown."

One of the reasons I admired Pillsbury was that I knew exactly where he was from, and understood how hard it must have been to rise above his circumstances. Even now, hidden away in our hills, families eke out a hardscrabble existence in roofed-over cellars, where a boy or girl with any spirit would be crushed by poverty and indifference; to have one of these young people go on to college is all but unknown, and to have one of them then go on to become a leader in a great movement would be a miracle. Pillsbury did just that. He became a paid (poorly paid) grassroots field organizer for Garrison's American Anti-Slavery Society, going town to town, church to church, fighting the religious establishment that tried to censor the abolitionist message—and it took a special kind of man to do this well.

Emerson, for one, was much impressed:

> Pillsbury, who I heard last night, is the very gift from New Hampshire which we have long expected, a tough oak stick of a man not to be silenced or insulted or intimidated by a mob, because he is more mob than they; he mobs the mob. John Knox is come at last, on whom neither money nor politeness nor hard words nor rotten eggs nor kicks and brickbats make the slightest impression. He is fit to meet the bar-room wits and bullies; he is a wit and a bully himself and something more; he is a graduate of the plough and cedar swamp and snowbank, and has nothing new to learn of labor or poverty or the rough of farming.

Courage and strength are qualities he would need. As his biographer Stacey M. Robertson relates, "During one meeting at Cape Cod, Pillsbury was ejected from the platform with many 'kicks and blows,' by a 'ferocious mob,' which then 'dashed the platform all to pieces.' In the course of the attack, the abolitionists had their clothes literally torn all to shreds."

Years of braving this kind of abuse could exhaust an activist. "'A hard, stern life!' one field agent testified. 'Does anyone wish to become an iceberg, or a granite rock?—to become stern, severe as death?—to become hard, impervious, forbidding, repulsive?—let him enter the Anti-Slavery conflict!'"

Pillsbury traveled to Europe to proselytize, came back for a brief reunion with his family in New Hampshire, then carried his abolitionist message out West, putting up in squalid taverns or barns, holding his meetings in flour mills or lumberyards or wherever it was safe. It was immediate and unconditional emancipation he preached, under the famous Garrisonian motto, "No compromise!"

Pillsbury spent over twenty-five years at this kind of grunt work, and continued long after the Civil War, fighting not only for freeman rights, but rights for women (Susan B. Anthony admired him greatly); he kept traveling and lecturing in the 1890s, by which time all his former colleagues in the movement were dead. "I work like a man who is both farmer and blacksmith," he wrote once, in a forgivable moment of hard-won pride. "And an abolitionist and temperance man to boot, and whose wife keeps no maid. If you know any such, or ever did know such, and if they still survive, and hold fast the truth faith and form of Godliness, give them the everlasting respect, esteem and love of Parker Pillsbury."

ALBERT CAMUS

It's a sad but interesting phenomenon, this expedient of escaping your times by admiring heroes from the past. As the anger of the eighties turned to the passivity of the nineties ("Whatever," said with a dismissive shrug, was the buzzword of the day) and then to the horrors of the century's beginnings, I rediscovered someone whose moral authority and example had already made a huge impact on my life. Wars in Iraq, torture, terrorism, culture battles, materialism, greed. Like everyone, I needed to find an antidote, and, with few candidates on offer in contemporary life, I went back to a man whose courage, measured against the present, was astonishing: Albert Camus.

Once upon a time, everyone admired Camus, or pretended to; back in the sixties, if you had any pretensions to intellectual cool, you carried a copy of *The Stranger* under your arm, preferably in the original French. Trendy, sure, but there was real substance behind this—Camus was perhaps the last writer whose moral influence rivaled Tolstoy's or Dickens's. Certainly, there is no one like him today, so low in the visual/digital age has the status of serious literature fallen. Mailer and Lowell helped lead the March on the Pentagon in 1967, but who knows any poets or novelists anyone would follow today, and even if there were such, no one was marching, not during the second Bush years, when even those who bitterly hated the Iraq War didn't want to appear ungrateful to our troops. The influence of writers had fallen so low in the forty years since Camus died that you can only measure the drop by going back, and, with a bittersweet combination of nostalgia and awe, realizing again how gigantic a figure Camus had been.

The Stranger was the Camus I read first, and the flat existentialism seemed relevant, not so much to my condition just then, but to the current mood in life at large; when Meursault shoots the Arab on the beach, we can weirdly sympathize with the absurdity of the act, even when he shoots the dead body four times more—"and each successive shot was another loud, fateful rap on the door of my undoing." (Fascinating to think that Camus wrote the novel in 1942, during the Nazi occupation of France, though its overall mood says much more about the fifties and sixties; fascinating, too, is the novel's prescience—sixty years later, Meursault wasn't the only Westerner to be shooting Arabs for no good reason.)

The Plague is a much larger book—an allegory of the Occupation that is firmly rooted in realism, so the metaphors, the parallels, don't seem forced, but spring naturally out of the novel's closely observed Oran. And Camus isn't afraid to be explicit when it comes to spelling out his moral beliefs. Here, Tarrou, the drifter who finds his calling in caring for the sick, describes to Dr. Rieux his theory that if a man can't fight for freedom and liberty, he can at least avoid cooperating with the hangmen:

"I only know that one must do what one can to cease being plague-stricken, and that's the only way in which we can hope for some peace, or failing that, a decent death. This, and only this, can bring relief to men, and, if not save them, at least do them the least possible harm, and even, sometimes, a little good. So this is why I resolved to have no truck with anything which, directly or indirectly, for good reasons or bad, brings death to anyone or justifies others' putting him to death . . . The good man, the man who infects hardly anyone, is the man who has the few lapses of attention. Yes, Rieux, it's a wearying business, being plague-stricken. But it's still more wearying to refuse to be it."

Since Camus followed these dictates in his own life, his moral authority was immense. Justin O'Brien, his brilliant translator, is not exaggerating when he says, "Over and above intellectual or political leadership, he provided the moral guidance the postwar generation needed. By overcoming the immature nihilism and despair that he saw as poisoning our century, he emerged as the staunch defender of our positive moral values, and, in his own words, 'of those silent men, who, throughout the world, endure the life that has been made for them.' "

It's difficult for a contemporary novelist, all but completely disenfranchised, to look back on Camus's career without feeling envious—envious that fifty years ago, literature had such an exalted status that one of its practitioners could influence world opinion. Once you get past this, looking at Camus's work in detail, it's remarkable how relevant his writing remains. Everything about the AIDS epidemic—denial, lack of leadership, misinformation, hysteria, and, yes, courage—are all in *The Plague*. And if you think about that other plague, the moral sickness that took hold of this country during the Bush-Cheney years, the torture years, then that's in *La Peste*, too:

Rieux knew what those jubilant crowds did not know but could have learned from books: that the plague bacillus never dies or disappears for good; that it can lie dormant for years and years in furniture and in linen chests; that it bides its time in bedrooms, cellars, trunks and bookshelves; and that perhaps the day would come when, for the bane and the enlightening of men, it would rouse up its rats again and send them forth to die in a happy city.

Admiring Camus so much, I was pleased to learn that he greatly admired three of my own heroes: Melville, Thoreau, and Emerson. That he should admire the first is no surprise—Melville's brave, unflinching despair is very much in the Camus mode—but that he should also admire Emerson and Thoreau's optimism is not something you would expect.

Here he is on Melville:

> His admirable books are among those exceptional works that can be read in different ways, which are at the same time both obvious and obscure; the wise man and the child can both draw sustenance from them . . . *Moby-Dick* can be seen as one of the most overwhelming myths ever invented on the subject of man against evil, depicting the irresistible logic that finally leads the just man to take up arms first against creation and the creator, then against his fellow man and against himself . . . Melville's genius and the sovereignty of his work bursts with health, strength, explosions of humor, and human laughter. His anguished books in which man is overwhelmed, but in which life is exalted on every page, are inexhaustible sources of strength and pity.

As for the Transcendentalists, Camus quotes them when he talks about how tempting it is for the artist to "surrender" by giving up that which is most precious—his faith in himself. Camus: " 'A man's obedience to his own genius,' Emerson said magnificently, 'is faith in its purest form.' And as Thoreau added, 'So long as a man is faithful to himself, everything is in his favor, government, society, the very sun, moon and stars.' "

Then, in trying to describe the challenges a novelist faces in describing a tormented world, Camus quotes Emerson again: " 'Every wall is a door.' "

The essay in which these quotes appear is my favorite of Camus's writings, and a cornerstone of my own literary faith: "Create Dangerously," a lecture he gave to university students in Sweden in 1957. It isn't as well known as his Nobel Prize acceptance speech of three years later, but it's one of the most courageous statements of artistic courage we have. I was surprised and not surprised, going back to read it again last night, how many paragraphs I remembered by heart.

"Create Dangerously"—the title alone was enough to inspire me. It was 1969 when I read it first; Camus's delineation of the dilemmas and challenges facing writers still seemed burningly relevant. On one hand, writers were being asked to write for the masses and join the Communists; on the other, they were offered a privileged ivory-tower life if they forgot mankind's sufferings and went along with the bourgeois West. Camus knew what this tension was like, and the more specifically French dilemma of whether to give his moral support to the freedom fighters in Algeria (who were killing people he grew up with), or the paratroopers who were repressing them (and killing people he grew up with). In his great essay, Camus bravely fights his way toward an answer—and becomes one of those rare writers who ends up praising the principled middle ground. "The artists can never turn away from his time, nor lose himself in it—he can never escape from this ambiguity."

I'll say it again: Reading Camus now, in the early years of this century, makes you weep for the fallen state of literature—the dilemmas Camus outlines seem almost quaint. But there is much in the essay that speaks to me as directly and powerfully now as it did then, since Camus doesn't just talk about the writer's political role, but goes to the very heart of literature's purpose:

> The greater an artist's revolt against the world's reality, the greater can be the weight of reality to balance that revolt. The loftiest work will always be, as in the Greek tragedians, Melville, Tolstoy and Molière, the work that maintains an equilibrium between reality and man's rejection of that reality, each forcing the other upward in a ceaseless overflowing, characteristic of life itself at its most joyous and heart-rending

extremes. Then, every once in a while, a new world appears, different from the everyday world and yet the same, particular, but universal, full of innocent insecurity—called forth for a few hours by the power and longing of genius. The world is nothing and the world is everything—that is the contradictory and tireless cry of every true artist, the cry that keeps him on his feet with his eyes open, and that, every once in a while, awakens for all in this world the fleeting and insistent image of a reality we recognize without ever having known it.

Create dangerously. He's defining the title now, working toward his inspiring conclusion:

Beauty has never enslaved anyone. And for thousands of years, every day, at every second, it has instead assuaged the servitude of millions of men and women, and, occasionally, liberated some of them once and for all . . . The greatness of art lies in the perpetual tension between beauty and pain, the love of men and the madness of creation, unbearable solitude and the exhausting crowd, rejection and consent. Art advances between two chasms, which are frivolity and propaganda. On the ridge where the great artist moves forward, every step is an adventure, an extreme risk. But if art is not an adventure, what is it and where is its justification?

If art is not an adventure, what is its justification? Put that on Camus' headstone. Or put down another of his lines, which is either the boldest statement he ever made, or perhaps the most humble: "Artists are the only people who never harmed the world."

STAN ROGERS

Old admirations still meant a lot to me, but I remained on the hunt for new ones as the millennium ebbed and turned. New to me was Ivo Andric, the Bosnian-Serb writer whose deeply imagined, closely observed novels about the Balkans explained better than any journalist what the clash of cultures there was all about; Tom Toles, *The Washington Post* political cartoonist, whose courageous humor helped pull me through the Bush-Cheney years; Stan Rogers, the Canadian singer-songwriter who I discovered just before his far-too-early death.

Rogers looked like a sea captain, and sang like one, too, with the kind of deep baritone voice that could cut through hurricane squalls, and then, the storm clouds breaking, croon a ballad to the brightly emergent moon. He made his songs out of subjects no one else thought of touching—displaced exiles from the Maritimes forced to move west to find jobs; second-generation Canadian-Irish refusing to get drawn into Ireland's troubles; Sir John Franklin searching for the Northwest Passage; a middle-aged salesman remembering when he was a young hockey star. In his beautifully wistful "Lies," a farm wife on the prairies looks into the mirror and wonders where her youth has gone; in "Tiny Fish for Japan," cannery workers on the Great Lakes lament the passing of the fisheries on which their livelihood depended; in "Barrett's Privateers," a young sailor profanely rues the day he ever left Nova Scotia.

A decided theme in Rogers's work, one that spoke to me very strongly, is the virtue and necessity of second effort. Perhaps his best song, "The *Mary Ellen Carter*," tells the story of a fishing-boat crew who, after the boat sinks in a storm, vows to raise it off the bottom and start over—a song that stirringly widens its message at the very end. "To you to whom adversity had dealt the final blow / with smiling bastards lying to you everywhere you go / Turn to and put out all your strength of arm and heart and brain / and like the *Mary Ellen Carter*, rise again!"

Refusing to quit in a more personal sense is the theme of "Turnaround," with a line, "It's harder to start again than it was to begin," that seemed, with where I was then in my career, intended just for me.

A sad day, the morning when the flight he was aboard caught fire in Cincinnati. For Stan Rogers's many admirers, the day the music died.

I'm writing the last pages of this book in the winter after my sixtieth birthday, and I'm aware most of all how many there are who, like Stan Rogers, I won't have time to give the proper attention to, but who have somewhere along the way inspired me, consoled me, encouraged me, entertained me, challenged me, or, in other words, did those precious, never-to-be-forgotten things that admirer-ees do for admirers.

For instance:

Robert McCloskey, whose books I loved as a boy, not just *Blueberries for Sal*, but his "Homer Circle" stories. Art Carney—his Ed Norton in *The Honeymooners* is still my favorite TV character. Bob Cousy, "Cooz," whose around-the-back passes and elegant push shot my generation of basketball players grew up trying to imitate. Theodore Bikel, Mary Martin's costar in *The Sound of Music*, a thinking-man's folksinger. Audie Murphy, the small-town boy who became the most decorated GI in World War II, and later starred in war movies and Westerns. Maria Tallchief, the famous Native American ballerina. George Meade, the Union commander at Gettysburg, who I always felt got a raw deal from history—he won there, didn't he? Steve Allen, "Steverino," smart and funny, the man who invented the talk show (which I don't hold against him). Bill Mauldin, cartoonist of *Willie and Joe*, the weary dogfaces. Dr. Benjamin Spock—not just the baby doctor who helped our parents raise us, but the brave political activist who took seriously his duty to protect and to heal. Rachel Carson, who I read early. Paul Siple, the "Boy Scout with Byrd" in Antarctica. Roy White, the underrated left-fielder who was the last New York Yankee I ever bothered caring about. Jonas Salk—the man who kept me and my friends from catching polio.

Those are for starters, the heroes I worshipped when I was just starting to learn what admiration was all about. After that came my golden age, my twenties and thirties, with a list that could be ten times longer than what I'll have room to sketch here. Eudora Welty, a writer who taught me a lot about seriousness of literary purpose. Marcel Proust—reading Proust was one of the great intellectual adventures of my life. Arthur Rubinstein, who I saw give his last concert ever, when he was well up in his eighties; appearing at a gala with the New York Philharmonic, he played a Beethoven piano concerto followed by the Brahms Second, followed by two Chopin encores—and seemed as fresh and energized at the end as at the beginning. Eastman Johnson's idyllic watercolors made me weep for our vanished past. Vera Brittain wrote a masterpiece of World War I, *Testament of Youth*, and led a life dedicated to peace and reconciliation. Nadezhda Mandelstam wrote one of the greatest books of the twentieth century, *Hope Against Hope*, about how she fought to save her poet husband from death in Stalin's camps.

Nathanael West I'd have to include—his *Miss Lonelyhearts* made a huge impression, and *The Day of the Locust* hit me even harder. Aldo Leopold, the great conservationist, I read again and again. I owned every Paul Robeson recording I could get my hands on. Henry Roth's *Call it Sleep* was on my top-ten novel list, and I understood why, after having it received in total indifference, he moved to Maine and became a chicken farmer. Th'ch Quang Duc was the Buddhist monk whose self-immolation in 1963 was the first brave protest that caused many to understand that our Vietnam involvement was all wrong.

Alexander Solzhenitsyn stands very high, and I felt a strong personal connection, knowing he lived not that far south of me in Vermont. Neil Gunn's novels set in Scotland were mostly unknown in the States, but I went out of my way to find them. Aaron Copland I've always admired—and what nice irony, that a gay Jewish New York intellectual captured better than anyone the strong, rhythmic harmonies of the American West. Janet Baker, the British contralto, I saw sing four or five times at Carnegie Hall, and there was something truly majestic about her voice and presence. I went through a Katherine Mansfield phrase, read all her stories and journals. Sherwood Anderson meant a lot to me, as did Ring Lardner and F. Scott Fitzgerald. Ivan Bunin was the next-to-last of the great Russian short-story writers, and the very last, Isaak Babel, I admired also.

The list grew longer after my kids grew up—when it came to admiration, I suddenly had more free time to look around and shop. New admirations included Willie Nelson, the left-leaning country singer (!). John Muir, whose rapturously lyrical nature writings I only found my way to after a visit to Yosemite. Jimmy Carter, the president who grew so much as a man after leaving the White House, and whose sincere and generous faith made me decide that not all believers were hypocrites. Paul Scholes, the latest of the sports stars I admired like a kid does—"Scholesy," the clever midfielder on the great Manchester United teams of the early century. Cindy Sheehan, the mother who lost her son in Iraq and bravely spoke out against the war. Private Harry Patch, wounded at the Battle of Passchendaele in 1916, and still alive and well ninety-two years later.

And finally, there are those who I can only list as names—but how eloquently the list speaks to me! Johnny Cash. Charles Schulz. Cesar Chavez. Bill Bradley. Charles Ives. Edward Abbey. Paul Strand. Robert Ryan. Kathe Kollwitz. Michael Caine. Roger Tory Peterson. Peter Sellers. Jean Sibelius. John Gunther. Anna Akhmatova. Tom Paine. Abbey Lincoln. Bob Keeshan. Primo Levi. Helen Caldicott. David Souter. Red Cloud. H. W. Tilman. Nelson Mandela. William Sloane Coffin. Billy Bragg. Gabriel Garcia Marquez. Linus Pauling. Alan Hovhaness. Robert Capa. Max Roach. Walker Evans. Emma Goldman. Charles Cotton. Gordon Lightfoot. Roderick L. Haig-Brown.

"We live by admiration, hope and love," Wordsworth insisted, and he could have had the young person I once was as his model. Hope I was born with, love found its way to me, but admiration I learned entirely on my own. In a life short on mentors, I had to go out and find mine where I could; culture at large sometimes helped in this, but just as often hindered, creating so many false gods to worship that it almost always missed the true ones, the ones who would make a difference. But that's the great thing—how I didn't need anyone to teach me to admire, but took those first tentative baby steps all by myself.

Admiration took a shy, introspective boy living in the blandest suburb imaginable and widened his world enough so that he could breathe; it bought him time and space in which to become who he needed to become, when without it his spirit would have been flattened and perhaps even crushed. Admiration gave him secret friends when he scarcely had any real ones. Admiration made him raise his standards when all the other forces working on him tended to lower those standards. Admiration made him aware of a tradition of human fortitude and excellence that he wanted more than anything to become part of himself.

Admiration taught him to admire quiet excellence. Admiration, in a worldview that tended to be jaundiced, saved him from jaundice. All of us, even the least thoughtful, constantly sit in judgment over mankind, and if the young man often became too harsh in this, too quick and damning, admiration was there to soften his verdicts, and for this alone he had to be grateful.

There are gaps, looking back. As hard as I did fight, I should have struggled harder to burst free of the cultural assumptions that were out there working on me in ways I hardly understood at the time. I should have gone out and found more women to admire, more blacks and Latinos; I should have found more heroes from the world of science, instead of condemning them all as A-bomb makers and crazy Frankensteins. I'm sure there were architects creating brave, human-scale buildings that would have greatly inspired me, but I never learned their names, saw their masterpieces; there must have been mathematicians whose discoveries were miracles of human ingenuity and imagination, but, if there were, no one told me about them, and, if they had, the ability to comprehend it all was strictly for specialists. And gangsters—how come I never fell for one, like most Americans? There were always more cultural and generational biases working on me than I was ever aware of, and while my path was broader than most, it was still a path; I could only chop with my machete so far before I had to come back.

The moment I finish writing, I intend to go back and count the names I've listed here—not just those admirable figures I've celebrated, but the ones I've mentioned just in passing. Whatever the number turns out to be, I could easily suck in my breath and triple it. Putting these names down gives me the illusion that what I'm really doing is creating *one* human face, our best face—the one that shines brightest and bravest. Back at the beginning, I posed the question Emerson once asked: "Is the world upheld by the veracity of good men?" I sidestepped answering, and maybe now have to sidestep again.

Is mankind admirable? Often no, sometimes yes. Blend my heroes with yours, add in the quiet ones, the uncelebrated and unknown, who, by the courage and patience of their lives define human dignity, and together we can make our appeal.

Epilogue

BARACK OBAMA

A cold January morning in western New Hampshire. It's not snowing, but it may as well be, the grayness is so damp and chilling. A father and his seventeen-year-old son are searching for a place to park in the valley's one small city; on their third circuit of downtown, no spaces have yet opened. It's Monday, school is in session, but it's one of those rare days that the son has no trouble convincing his father are better spent outside the classroom than in. But now, noting the unusually large number of cars, sensing the presence of a crowd they haven't quite seen yet, the father has second thoughts.

"I know where we can park," he says. "Back at the high school."

His son laughs. "Nice try, Dad. Besides, I already called in sick."

"We preregistered for this, right? On the campaign's Web site?"

"Try a left up here." Then, a few seconds after they drive clear of downtown's largest, bulkiest bank, "Wow! Look at that!"

On an ordinary morning there might be four or five people walking quickly across the green on their way to work, but now, as they come into the open plaza outside the town's opera house, they see a line snaking back from the entrance all the way down the street, around the corner, past the gas-station pumps, down the next street past the senior citizen center, and fifty yards further back than that.

The father, surprised and not surprised, is just about to say something when a UPS truck pulls away from the curb and a golden space opens up. That's step one—but step two looks to be impossible.

"No one's going to care we're preregistered," the father says. "We're talking two thousand people on that line."

His son remains optimistic. "Maybe we can cut in?"

They walk over to the opera house steps where the line begins. It's five abreast, tightly packed, friendly-looking—at least until the two of them come too close. Queue hopping is clearly out of the question. They walk slowly, reluctantly, toward the end of the line, hoping board. The angry had all the intensity, the good lacked all conviction, and people like me could do nothing about it but shrug their shoulders and paraphrase Yeats.

Needing relief from this, searching for an antidote, I came upon a whole class of admirable figures, albeit ones who had been dead a hundred years: the abolitionists. I went through a stage where I read every book on them I could find, looked up their writings, gloried in their passionate intensity that was—miracle upon miracle!—actually enlisted on the side of good.

Even with a serious, semiprofessional interest in American history, I'd not heard much about the abolitionists, probably because their constituency was constantly shrinking. Black pride was understandably touchy about white efforts to end slavery—wasn't it Harriet Beecher Stowe, after all, who had given us Uncle Tom?—and they were more apt to honor their own Frederick Douglass or Sojourner Truth. Feminists had their own historical fish to fry, and they neglected female abolitionists like the brave and rebellious Grimké sisters of Charleston, who would steal off to slave cottages at night to rub oil on the wounds of slaves who had been whipped: "The light was put out, the key-hole screened, and flat on our stomachs before the fire, we defied the laws of South Carolina." Feminists not only neglected them, but also the female antislavery societies that sprang up all over the North, giving American women, perhaps for the first time ever, a political cause they could organize around, and, in so doing, discover their own strength.

The South, a hard-core part of it, remains pissed about the Civil War's outcome, and since populous markets like Texas control the textbook industry, little Johnny isn't apt to read about abolitionists in school. Even in the North, abolitionists are often conflated with the Radical Republicans, or treated as madmen on the order of John Brown.

The fact I had to discover them on my own only increased my admiration once I found them. And what a relief it was, to admire angry men and women who were angry for the right reasons! There was Theodore Parker, the Massachusetts clergyman whose inspirational sermons and speeches gave the antislavery movement its soul; John Greenleaf Whittier, the Quaker poet of Haverhill, Massachusetts, someone they know will call out to them and drag them in. No one does. Campaign workers scurry about on the flanks of the crowd, excited, happy, useless, and when the father waves a copy of their preregistration at one of them, she shakes her head.

"Only the first eight hundred get inside," she says. "We're trying to arrange for the senator to speak to everyone who can't get in from the steps."

The father and son join the end of the line, do a rough count of heads, realize it's hopeless. The father has given up a morning's work, the son has skipped class, and not on a casual whim, but to witness history. Drastic measures are called for, even if they border on unethical—even if they cross the border. The two of them walk to the head of the line, notice among those waiting in the second dozen a young man the father once coached in youth basketball. Not exactly a friend, but close enough.

"Hey, Jack!" the son calls out—and just like that, the two of them are standing next to him, making small talk, doing their best to act inconspicuous. Jack accepts their presence with his usual placid smirk. More important, the ones waiting on line just behind accept their presence, too. A second later the opera house doors open, and then ten seconds after that, the father and son are seated three rows back from the stage, under the impassive, stereo gaze of what have to be the two tallest, baddest-looking Secret Service agents in the country.

Lebanon's opera house is a very New Hampshire kind of place, a very American place. Like many similar opera houses across the country, it was built in the 1890s, when a prosperous middle-class family had time to indulge in some culture—maybe not opera, but vaudeville performances and Chautauqua lecturers and whatever else was wandering the countryside promising some laughs and/or some education.

Graduations could be held there in a pinch if it rained; town meetings every March filled the seats with cranky voters, while, out in the lobby, the Ladies' Aid sold cider donuts and maple cream pie. As the decades wore on, the opera house became neglected, then derelict, then moldy—but then in the eighties, a group of civic-minded people got together and spruced it up, with new paint, new seats, new lighting, and new attitude. Famous acts were booked—Joan Baez, Sweet Honey in the Rock, Garrison Keillor—and, biggest miracle of all, a professional opera company was established, "North Country Opera," with summer performances that drew fans from all over New England. Almost a century after it was constructed, the opera house became a real opera house after all.

So far this winter, during New Hampshire's first-in-the-nation primary, three Republican candidates for the presidential nomination have spoken here, and seven of the eight Democrats. The last of these, the eighth, is about to make his entrance. Everyone is standing up, facing not the stage, but the doors to the lobby, where there's a hip-hopping kind of flash and swarm. Cameras point that way, aides hurry over with their clipboards, and the reporters, at least forty of them (trying to look blasé and not managing to), get up from their reserved seats to see what's happening. Just like the aide promised, the senator is standing outside on the opera house steps speaking to those who can't get inside—and even through the thick doors and granite walls, their cheers can be felt, so those inside, excited already, now begin spontaneously applauding, responding, not to the candidate's words (which can't be heard), but to the buzz and throb.

With this kind of buildup, the candidate should burst through the doors and prance down the aisle, slapping hands all the way to the stage. But no. Running in the New Hampshire primary is hard work, and he needs time to collect himself backstage, sip some coffee, gather his thoughts. There's a lull of twenty minutes, but no one seems to mind. The reporters fan out through the auditorium with their microphones and notepads, and one of them, perhaps on the hunt for craggy, weather-beaten New Hampshire types, descends on the father and fires away.

"What'd he ask you?" the son says, after he leaves.

"Who I'm voting for and why."

"What did you tell him?"

"That I was tired of being cynical when it comes to politicians. That I'm ready to be post-cynical."

The son points to the empty podium. "Do you think he's going to win?"

Interesting, the tone he uses. It's not like a favorite sports team he's asking about; he's asking like he's a little kid again, and wants his father to reassure him when he's been injured or scared. But this is American politics, not a boo-boo on the knee, and all his father can do is shrug.

"God only knows. But I'm optimistic."

A lot of people in the opera house must feel that way, judging by the eager, excited way they wait. Young people especially. There are dozens of them. Area schools must think they've been hit by a sudden outbreak of the flu, and if teenagers view the candidate as some kind of rock star or Hollywood celebrity, then fine—that's the way they respond to politicians now, and the smarter ones will get past that and listen closely to what he has to say.

There are risers on the stage, the rolling, portable kind you might have in a gym for basketball; a diverse (for New Hampshire) group of voters take their seats there, forming a photogenic semicircle around the podium where the candidate will stand. A portly, friendly-looking man walks to the microphone and introduces himself. The owner of a local Mexican restaurant, he's a veteran of Iraq, the father of three children, and he's here to explain why, after not voting in the last two elections, he's voting in this one.

He does well with his speech; it projects honesty and hope, and if he hesitates a split second before pronouncing the candidate's name, all of us are still in that stage, where it doesn't trip naturally off the tongue.

"The next President of the United States, Bar-ack . . . Obama!"

The crowd erupts. A lithe young man comes out onstage; both the father and son immediately notice (they'll tell each other this later in the car) that he walks like a point guard coming back to the bench after a great first half; there's a prance in his walk, a hint of a strut. The father has the disorienting reaction he always has when seeing someone in person he's only seen in newspapers or on TV—My god, he's real after all!—but this quickly dissipates, and he can focus more soberly on his features.

His ears are big, the cartoonists have that right, but the noticeable gauntness in his cheeks, rather than making him appear weak, suggests strength and compassion. He looks smart, alert, sensitive; unusually for a male face, his intelligence seems centered in his lips, which purse and relax, purse again, relax, in emphasis to his words. The way he waves to the audience, nods, tries to talk through the applause, backs away from the microphone, laughs, starts again, suggests a crisp, business-like amiability. He wears a tie, a white shirt, no jacket; his sleeves are rolled up, ready to work. The costume of a caring, man-of-the-people American politician circa 2008, but there's nothing routine or cliché about the man wearing it, and the longer the father stares at him, the more the difference sinks in.

The crowd finally quiets. He begins his speech.

The father would give a lot to trade places with his son right now, to better know what he is experiencing. As for what the father experiences himself, listening to the senator talk, it's the kind of half-physical, half-mental response that's difficult to describe.

It's earthy and tactile more than intellectual and abstract. There's an unlocking or unclenching sensation that comes very fast, and which can only be from his cynicism dissolving, or at least starting to melt. A blush is involved, too—a boyish blush, the kind that burned his cheeks as a kid when he met an adult he badly wanted to have notice and like him. Hope is there, too, and not just in the abstract, but the kind you feel in your gut when you're expecting good news and it's a second before it's delivered. And trust—a calming, soothing sensation, working on his overly developed, overworked muscle of doubt. Connoisseurship kicks in, an appreciation that settles like a *frisson* down the back of his neck; this man, compared to hundreds of others listened to over many years, speaks well, really well. Most striking of all in the response is a surge of youth, as if, quite literally, vigor has been shot in the father's arm all the way from the podium.

A writer, a man obsessed with finding the right words, he tries to give these complex sensations a unifying name, and, after quickly running through the candidates, he realizes there is only one possibility: *admiration*. It's admiration that he feels as he listens to the young senator talk. Admiration not just for him, but—in a generous kind of overflow emotion—for the people behind him on the stage, and the people sitting in the opera house applauding, and his son getting to his feet and cheering next to him, and the men in charge of the lighting and sound, the reporters in back, the Secret Service agents and the campaign aides, and, for that matter, opening the doors now, the entire state of New Hampshire, all of New England, the U.S. of A., the United States of Admiration—admiration, the strongest jolt he's felt in a long time, and he's lost in it, and, even if it's fated not to last very long, it feels absolutely wonderful to be lost there, after being trapped inside so many crabbier moods for the last eight years.

Everyone in the audience must feel this, or similar emotions. Everyone out there past the doors. "Yes we can!" they start chanting, as Barack Obama finishes, turns to shake hands with the people behind him, turns back again to wave. "Yes we can! Yes we CAN! YES WE CAN—" . . . and maybe it's only the father who notices the hyphen that invisibly hangs on the chant's end, and seems waiting for just the right word to top it off. Can—*what?* End torture? Stop the wars? Save our planet? Fix health care? Rescue the middle class? Yes, it's all those things, but there's a more-immediate need they're adding on like an exclamation point, without explicitly realizing it or pronouncing it, but putting it there just the same—a word they haven't been permitted in what seems like generations . . . the word ADMIRE! written in caps and underlined and printed as boldly as can be.

PETE SEEGER

Two months later I'm back at the opera house again. I haven't cut into the line this time, but paid for a ticket, and never was $50 better spent. Pete Seeger is giving a benefit concert to support local farmers—Pete Seeger, my boyhood hero; Pete Seeger, who I haven't seen perform in almost forty years; Pete Seeger, who is eighty-nine years old. If "legendary" was the word people put before his name in 1968, what adjective could possibly do him justice now? The "immortal" Pete Seeger? The "eternal" Pete Seeger?

"He's outlasted all his critics," is something often said of him, but it's become more triumphant than that now. Seeger, of all things he might yet be in his career, is *hot.* One of his admirers, Bruce Springsteen, has a hit album with exuberant rock updates of Seeger favorites. A new documentary profile, *The Power of Song,* is winning rave reviews. A grassroots petition drive is under way to nominate him for the Nobel Peace Prize. The San Diego school board has issued him a formal apology for having prohibited him from singing in their high school forty years ago. Eight months from the night of this concert, two days before Barack Obama's inauguration, Seeger will sing "This Land is Your Land" before the president-elect and 500,000 people on the steps of the Lincoln Memorial, closing the afternoon's show. A few months after that, celebrating his ninetieth birthday, he will sell out Madison Square Garden a half-hour after tickets go on sale—and anyone who knew his story, where he had come from, how much courage and faith he had poured into life, must have been crying to think that, after keeping hope alive so long with his music, his story had the happy ending it so emphatically deserved.

The opera house is crowded with people my age, but some much older, and a good sprinkling of kids. We've come to worship, of course, but Pete is having none of that. He walks briskly out onstage carrying his banjo, seems startled to see so many of us, smiles, cups his hands around his eyes like binoculars to peer out into the lights, swings his banjo around behind his back so he can applaud *us*, swings the banjo back again, strums a few chords, hums, then starts right in.

"Well may the world go, the world go, the world go. Well may the world go, when I'm far away."

Seeger probably looked venerable when he was nine, let alone eighty-nine, so, while his beard is whiter, time hasn't done much to his face. He still favors those outlandishly bright homespun shirts he wore last time I saw him; the one he wears tonight is a flowery red, tucked into trim jeans tapered down to the kind of running sneakers favored by active seniors. His famous Adams apple is as prominent as ever, especially when he cranes his head back and sings for what seems the last rows alone. (Seeger *always* sang to the back rows, ever aware of those in the cheapest seats.)

His grandson and a young blues singer share the stage with him, and when it comes their turn to solo, he sits on a stool, leans forward, and listens in rapt attention—and this is characteristic of him, too, the way he's so willing to sit and admire. (I've never realized this until now, when I'm thinking about the subject hard; one of the reasons I've admired Seeger so much over the years is because he is so good at admiration himself. Watch a tape of him when a protégé is singing with him, someone like Arlo Guthrie, Holly Near, or Bernice Reagon—his face positively glows. He's surely the best admirer I've ever seen, in a class by himself.)

He doesn't sit still for long. Somewhere toward the middle of their songs, he picks up the banjo, starts strumming, then humming, and then he's on his feet singing with them; he can't help it, the music takes control. At one point, he even breaks out into a little dance—well, no, not a little dance, a *real* dance. He's hopping back and forth like in the old days, performing "Abiyoyo." While his grandson sings, he keeps one weather eye on Pete, making sure everything is okay, and you can tell Pete is aware of this and grateful, but he can manage perfectly well on his own, thank you very much. Once, maybe twice, he forgets a lyric, makes a joke of it, but the words quickly come back; his banjo—across which his fingers youthfully fly—seems to find the words for him. And why shouldn't it? He had poured a lot into that banjo over the years, and now it was time for the white drum of it, the long fretted neck, to give back.

He's soon up to his old trick of getting everyone in the audience to sing along with him. "I'm not going to sing unless you do," he says, or "This only sounds good if we get a good chorus going," or, "There's no such thing as a wrong note as long as you're singing it," or, "Any high tenors out there?", then "Can't hear you!" The one that sounds best is "Amazing Grace"—not the pop, feel-good song it's become now, but the original version, the sternly beautiful antislavery song of the 1820s. We do a good job on this; Pete gets a bass line going, waves in our sopranos and altos, makes a pumping gesture to bring up the baritones, until finally there seems to be three distinct, slightly-behind-each-other melodies going all at once—but that's fine; it creates an echo-chamber effect off the opera house walls, and never has a song rung truer.

He follows this up with a song about Martin Luther King, Jr., then his famous "Turn Turn Turn," then, with everyone joining in again, the song he will sing (though he can't possibly guess this now) eight months later on the steps of the Lincoln Memorial: his pal Woody Guthrie's alternate national anthem, "This Land Is Your Land."

Watching, listening, singing, I feel many of the same sensations I experienced listening to Barack Obama, only on an older, more venerable level. My cynicism not only slackening, but disappearing completely, going off to a corner where it can damn well sulk without me. Hope rushing in to take its place. Connoisseurship—yes, his rapport with an audience is as strong as ever, and he sounds better in person than on his recent recordings. Trust—he's not someone who has ever let me down; for fifty years I've been admiring this man. Part of what this makes me feel is certainly nostalgia, but not the sentimental or sticky kind, since what I'm aware of most is a bittersweet contradiction about time that only someone my age or older can appreciate—that a half-century is simultaneously a long time ago and a split second ago; the two moments coexist.

The boy that once went to Carnegie Hall with his parents to listen to Pete Seeger could be on another planet, he seems so distant. The boy that once went to Carnegie Hall to see Pete Seeger could be sitting in the next seat, he seems so close.

And yes, "This Land Is Your Land" sounds a little bit nostalgic, a bit wistfully defiant, Pete singing it that night—the past trying its best to be heard by a modern era that is deaf. But a lot can happen in eight months. When I hear him sing that song next, on television from the Lincoln Memorial steps, it sounds completely different, a song that means something again—the present singing to the future and getting the future to sing along.

"How Can I Keep from Singing?" is the title of one of Seeger's most ardent, deeply felt songs. Thinking of him singing at those senior citizen gatherings near home, those fund-raisers for every cause imaginable, the local Labor Day picnics, croaking away on songs that must get harder and harder for him to remember, his fingers stiff but sure on the strings of his five string banjo, you have to answer the question very simply—that he *can't* keep from singing, and nothing in the horrors, defeats, and disappointments of his century ever made him stop.

He finishes the song with us. There's a standing ovation, an encore, and when he leaves the stage a final time, none of us move; we're unwilling to let the evening go. Somewhere toward the back rows, a feminine humming sound starts that we in the front only gradually realize is actual singing. The lyrics and melody become more distinct as the closer rows take it up, men join in, kids catch the words, until finally the whole opera house, the very walls, throbs to that old Weavers lullaby we all know so well.

"Good-night, Irene," we all sing. "Good-night, Irene. We'll see you in our dreams."